BETTER VIDEOS

STAND OUT. BE SEEN. CREATE CLIENTS.

RACHEL DUNN

CONTENTS

Foreword	vii
Introduction	ix
1. My Story	1
2. The Girl Director Solution Framework	22
3. The Big Picture	27
4. Audience Connection	41
5. Using Video for Marketing	51
6. Create Clients	63
7. Sabotaging Success	71
8. Be the ROCKSTAR of Your Message	75
9. Making Stand-Out Videos	81
10. The Ripple Effect	100
Acknowledgments	105
About the Author	109
Thank You	111
Want More Help	113

Copyright © Rachel Dunn, 2015

Version 2.0, 2021

All rights reserved. No part of this book may be reproduced in any form without permission in writing from the author. Reviewers may quote brief passages in reviews.

ISBN: 978-0-646-83653-9

DISCLAIMER

No part of this publication may be reproduced or transmitted in any form or by any means, mechanical or electronic, including photocopying or recording, or by any information storage and retrieval system, or transmitted by email without permission in writing from the author.

Neither the author nor the publisher assumes any responsibility for errors, omissions, or contrary interpretations of the subject matter herein. Any perceived slight of any individual or organization is purely unintentional.

Brand and product names are trademarks or registered trademarks of their respective owners.

Cover Design: Rachel Dunn

Editing: Grace Kerina

Cover photo courtesy of Viv Scanu

Author's photo on About the Author page courtesy of Wendy McDougall

Other images: Girl Director

For the most beautiful, spirited best friend in the world, Michael Hole, who has never stopped believing in me. From one crazy idea to the next, he has been right here by my side and he is here today as I write this book. He saw a vision on the day we met that we would be spending lots of time together watching videos. There are no words to describe how it feels to have a partner who sees me bigger than I see myself, a partner to share life experiences with, create a business with, and work with to help amazing clients around the world. Without a doubt, Michael has helped me become the person I am today. I know that without his love and support I wouldn't be writing this book.

And to Theo, our gorgeous Russian Blue who passed away a couple of months ago. I always saw him as an intelligent cat who preferred reading. He never liked the camera and preferred to be pondering and looking out for us. Since he's been gone, he's shown up in so many different ways, including while I've been writing this book. Theo has guided us and helped me to expand and connect to my heart instead of my head while writing this book.

FOREWORD

This is an inspiring, heartfelt, practical guide for helping women entrepreneurs find the missing ingredient for making better videos. It includes advice no technical manual could tell you, no class could teach you, and that no video production crew would give you. If you want your videos to stand out, if you want people to find you and hear your message – even if you're a little afraid to be on camera – this book is a must-read. Rachel has been passionate about video since she was in her teens, and her own inspiring story is in this book. Her encouragement shines throughout this book to show you that when you live your passion, you can use video to change the world, to change people's lives, and to make a difference. This is a book for anyone looking to make their own videos and make a bigger difference in the world. I have had the pleasure of working with Rachel on many film shoots and I've been greatly inspired by her original thinking, passion, enthusiasm, and knowledge.

Dr. Jim Frazier, OAM, ACS
Emmy Award Winner, Oscar Award Winner

INTRODUCTION

Life is like a camera: Focus on what's important, capture the good times,
develop from the negatives, and if things don't work out, take another shot.
Unknown

Have you ever watched behind the scenes documentaries of movies and thought, *I would love to make videos?* Are you finding yourself getting frustrated seeing other people's videos out there on social media? Are you feeling overwhelmed about where to start? Do you feel that the videos you've tried to make don't capture the true essence of who you are or reflect your message or what you're about?

You aren't alone.

Video has changed my life and has been my life for as long as I can remember. It's the perfect tool for making change, inspiring others, and growing your own confidence as you communicate your message. When you know how to make great videos, you'll become clearer in your communications and grow in ways you can't even imagine right now.

INTRODUCTION

I can't wait to share the fundamental things that will help you stand out, be seen, and make the difference you want to be making. I will warn you, though, that once you start making videos, your life will never be the same. Video is transformative in many ways. It helps boost your confidence, focus your message, grow your business, and connect you to your clients and the people around you. And you thought you were just buying a book about making better videos. Ha! A good video is so much more than just a video. I've watched women completely transform in front of my eyes when they start making videos and step into the person they truly want to be.

As you read this book, you'll begin looking at the world with your new Video Super Power. You'll see video locations and potential shots everywhere you turn. You'll see a video in everything. When you start making videos from the heart, people will contact you and want to know more about what you're up to, and you will feel so much more alive. You'll know you're making a difference.

In case you haven't noticed, there's a revolution going on with video. More and more women are starting to see its power and what happens when they fully embrace it.

Videos are sooooo addictive. I tell you, once you've been on a film set or a video shoot, you'll see there's nothing like it. Some of the best moments of my life have been when I was directing music videos on sets with 100 people walking around, all helping to create my vision and bring it to life! It's a pretty incredible feeling to create a finished video, all based on an idea you had. It's similar to writing a book.

The good news is that it's becoming easier and easier to make videos. I bet you'll be considering making a documentary or a movie in the not-too-distant future.

But before we jump ahead, let's start at the beginning.

INTRODUCTION

This book is designed to take you step by step through the exact process I use on every single video I make.

The Problem

The problem I see – and it's happening more and more with women entrepreneurs – is that there's so much pressure to stand out these days. There are thousands of women out there using video to monetize their businesses, get more leads, and find more clients. The problem is that there are, therefore, more people out there making videos that no one ever notices, videos that die a quiet, slow death. Which is really sad. You may be the best person out there at what you do, but if you don't communicate your message to your true audience, with your true voice, no one will notice you. It's like you're yelling and no one hears you.

If you're smart, like many of the people I work with, you've already realized that if you're going to invest time, money, and energy in making a video, then you need to make a video that stands out and attracts clients. Otherwise, what's the point, right?

I get it. You're doing more and more things with less time on your hands, and even the thought of learning how to make a great video right now overwhelms you. However, you're determined to find new ways to attract clients to your business – otherwise, you wouldn't be here. Plus, there's the added pressure of more and more social media applications out there to log on to and be seen on. Which ones do you choose? How do you stand out in today's rapidly expanding market? There are so many online platforms out there, and social media is only the tip of the iceberg.

There is also more and more competition out there. But you're a master at what you do and you want to help more people and be seen. You're sick of being invisible. So, the time for you to stand out is *now*.

INTRODUCTION

There is also so much free stuff available now that perhaps you're wondering if you're already too late. Perhaps you'll go to all this trouble and no one will be interested in what you have to say or want to watch your videos. Don't worry. All of the things you're feeling are completely normal. Every person I speak to about making a video has the same fears and thoughts.

I'll give you a tip: The more clearly you can visualize your videos in your mind before you create them, the better they'll be. In fact, this is exactly the same with your life vision. You are in the right place. You are exactly where you are meant to be right now. If you've been called to read this book, then please take notice and take action. My biggest successes have come from taking fast action. It can be scary, just like writing this book, but I choose to ignore the little negative voice telling me I can't do it, and just keep moving forward.

In today's busy world, there's less and less time to connect with your clients and potential customers – your audience. That's why this book is very important for you. You want to make sure you're spending your time on something that's going to make the biggest difference to your business and in the world.

Video is now the best way for you to make a difference. Imagine how exciting it would be if every businesswoman made a video to make a difference, to educate, and to inspire others!

The great thing is that people generally aren't using video to its full capacity. This is still the best-kept secret — and I'm going to let you in on it. Because you're ready to jump in and come on board for the ride now, I'm going to show you how to develop your very own Video Super Power.

* * *

INTRODUCTION

These are the *biggest* problems I see entrepreneurial women making online:

- Constant questioning and second guessing
- Tech overwhelm and don't know where to start
- Fear of getting it wrong
- Don't like the image they see looking back at themselves
- Poor quality videos that don't reflect their brand
- No Strategy
- Reactive to social media instead of responding
- Worry too much about what others think
- Distraction and lack of focus
- Lack of direction
- Don 't know how to engage with people using video
- Pay thousands to video production companies and don't get the desired results
- Don't know how to communicate using video

Does this sound like you?

After all, video is a *fun* platform, a form of creative expression. It's a tool to help you express yourself authentically and make the difference you want to be making. It will also help you to grow your business *fast*. (We'll go through how to make money with video a little later in the book, because there are some specific things you must do in order to make that happen.)

I want to warn you that if you're the kind of person who wants to get rich quick on YouTube, this book isn't for you. This book is about making videos that you're passionate about, that come from the heart, and that help you stand out. It's about making videos you're proud of. If you're confident about your videos, you'll want to share more. There's a higher

INTRODUCTION

vibrational energy that goes with things that you love. Every time I put out something I *love*, guess what? It's like a mirror. It reflects right back at me and attracts the things that I want, just like it did for Margaret...

Margaret's Story

Margaret is a public speaker, entrepreneur, and mentor. She's very confident when speaking in front of a room full of people, but when we put her in front of the camera, she froze and didn't feel like she was being her happy, fun, authentic self on screen.

She was very frustrated, because all her videos felt awkward. She didn't feel like the fun side of her personality came out. She was so hard on herself because she *knew* how to speak in front of a room; yet being on camera was awkward.

The biggest challenges for Margaret were not knowing where to start with making a better video, not feeling authentic, not understanding lighting and the techy stuff, and not seeing how video could help her develop her brand. She felt like every time she got on social media, she saw another person in her field with less experience doing better than she was doing and connecting to more clients than she had. The problem was that Margaret didn't have the technical know-how or experience to make videos that would stand out, and she didn't want to make herself look silly by putting out videos that weren't aligned with who she was.

Margaret felt like perhaps she shouldn't be the one to appear in her videos. She wasn't used to seeing her own image or hearing the sound of her voice. She thought she sounded different when she spoke.

She was so worried about the technical side that it blocked her ability to move forward. She'd had a bad experience with video in the past and wanted to make sure that this time, whatever she did worked.

Does this sound like you? Struggling with your image, worrying about your product, worrying that what you put out there in the world won't be aligned with who you are? Can you see how much it's costing you to worry about it over and over again instead of taking action to create what you want? By not adding video to your skill set, you're missing out on reaching the people you could be helping most.

What ended up happening for Margaret with video was simply inspiring. At 62 years old, she ended up loving it and embracing the technology. In fact, we have many clients in their 50s and 60s who are easily gaining the expertise to make their videos work.

Margaret started making lots of videos. She learned about editing and loved learning more. She was so enthusiastic about what was, for her, a new creative and expressive process.

We taught Margaret a new way to connect with clients – a way that's aligned with who she is. Since then, Margaret has created and marketed a video challenge on social media, launched a brand in alignment with who she is, and attracted new business leads and more VIP clients. And now she's added video-making as a new skill to share with her clients, which adds more value. She's had amazing results.

Margaret is authentic and fun on camera and she doesn't feel embarrassed anymore about what other people think. She's serving her clients in a much more profound way. She's found new ways to generate new clients through her video challenges and by building engagement.

The week Margaret committed to working with us and began implementing strategies around videos, she signed up her first VIP client. I was so inspired watching Margaret take everything on and implement everything we advised her to

INTRODUCTION

do. She took the guided action we offered and made it happen.

* * *

If any of Margaret's problems sound like what you're experiencing right now, know that this book will show you the way you, too, can be more authentic and make videos that speak to your market in a more profound way so that *you* stand out.

Over the coming chapters, you're going to learn how to grow in confidence and improve your communication. You'll also learn to love the things about yourself that perhaps you don't like now.

I know what you're thinking. But just you wait and see.

A Word on Technology

The first thing I want to do is change your mindset that you're terrible with technology, or that you and technology don't get along, or that you hate technology. I've seen this cripple people, including myself. If you go around thinking you aren't good with technology, then, guess what? You won't be good with technology.

There was a time when I hated my computer and everything I was doing. My brand new Macintosh computer had major issues and kept playing up, which was weird, because it was new and still under warranty. So I had it completely rebuilt – twice! The same problem still occurred. No one knew or could pinpoint what was wrong. The more if happened, the more frustrated I became.

Then I started to notice that everywhere I went, computers would play up and have technical issues. I told myself that I just had a thing with computers and wasn't very good with them. It got so bad that one day, when I was really stressed, a computer blew up next to me! I was incredibly

INTRODUCTION

stressed and unhappy at the time and working at a place where I was doing some contract work. It was weird that everywhere I went computers were having issues.

What stopped this pattern was a change in my attitude, in my mindset, and in my energy around computers. This all may sound a little woo woo, but it's true. As soon as I changed what I was thinking and feeling about computers, they changed. My computer that had been rebuilt twice started working. All my laptops started working again. It was like a curse had been lifted; the curse that was my attitude towards computers.

So, here's what I want you to do: Stop telling yourself you're no good with technology. It's time to embrace technology for what it can give you. Technology is the thing that is going to help propel you to the next level. Without it, you definitely won't reach the people you want to reach.

* * *

There's one thing I want to mention about the difference between Mac and PC computers. I understand that PCs are cheaper, but if you struggle with technology, Macs are probably going to be easier for you to use. They're built for designers who work with images and videos, so all of these features are built-in and make working on them so much easier and instinctive. I've used both Macs and PCs extensively and we recommend that all our clients who are struggling with technology look at buying a Mac. It's true: "Once you go Mac, you'll never go back."

Macs work easily with different files and have fewer problems with file formats. You can even look at getting one that has been reconditioned – a second-hand Mac is a great option.

INTRODUCTION

* * *

Please repeat this over and over again until you feel it's true: "Technology is easy. Technology is easy. Technology is easy." Even better, write out a whole page of that repeated phrase by hand – not on the computer. Even being aware of the mind chatter that goes on when you're thinking about using a computer is a step in the right direction.

Feel free to reach out to me if you need more help on this. I would love to hear about your experiences with technology, so email me your stories. Perhaps you had a light-bulb moment while reading my experience and you now realize that you can change your situation like I did! You can send emails to: iwantvideos@girldirector.com

MY STORY

You are the director of your videos and the director of your life.

I want to share a story with you now that I haven't ever shared in public, let alone in a book. Over the past 20-plus years I've had so many times of joy, terror, sadness, anger, and curiosity with video. Video has been like a best friend who's always been in my life. For as long as I can remember, I have held a camera.

Even though I knew I wanted to make videos, I had various fears and self-sabotaging beliefs that stopped me from moving forward as fast as I could have. Even with a plan, those layers of fears and doubts can get in the way. We often don't even know where they've come from.

To get to where I am today has taken years of self-development, reading books, working with mentors, and working hard to clear things that have been in the way of my success. The learning is a constant, too. I'm always clearing and noticing patterns that come up and bite me when I least expect them.

I've worked in many facets of video and TV, and have had many experiences that have led me to where I am today. I want to share them with you in the hope of inspiring you. Whatever crazy idea you have right now, you can do it!

Here's something to think about: It just takes 20 seconds of courage a day to change your life. What would you do right now if you had 20 seconds of courage to make a phone call or to do something to move you closer to your dreams? I live by this little rule when I want to propel myself to the next level. Try it now. Ask yourself what you would do right now if you had 20 seconds of courage.

Whatever you're going through and whatever is happening in your life, you can do this. Follow your instincts, follow your heart, and do those crazy things you've thought of but have been too afraid to do.

Video can open up new opportunities like you wouldn't believe. I'm here to inspire you to make those crazy ideas that you keep putting off happen, and I want you to let video help.

You're here for a reason. You have something you can do better than anyone else. It may seem like a little thing that's there hiding in the background – the thing you keep going back to that you would love to be doing if you had the money. That thing is what you want to tap into for making your videos.

I was one of those lucky people who knew exactly what they wanted to do when they grew up. I remember the exact moment: I was in grade eleven, sitting on the cream-colored carpet in my bedroom and blasting music out of my little cassette recorder. I was looking at a long list of career choices. I saw the word "cinematographer" on the career list my art teacher had given me. I was fascinated with the word and what it might mean, so I investigated. Not long afterwards, I came to the conclusion that I wanted to be a music video director.

It was like suddenly I just knew what I was here to do. I loved music and I loved video. I was obsessed with a band called INXS at the time and, like many teenagers, I was obsessed with music video clips. I watched everything to do with INXS. It was my dream to make a music video for them. That was my *big* dream goal. I used to visualize it and dream about what it would be like and how I would direct it. From then on, I was hooked on video.

After Michael Hutchence, the lead singer of INXS, passed away, I was devastated. It was like part of my dream died, too. I'd been so certain that I would create a video for them one day. However, I did have the opportunity to pitch a music video idea to the newly formed INXS a couple of years later and, wouldn't you believe it, the newly formed band broke up the week after my pitch!

I now have another goal for my music videos, which is very exciting. (I'll share more about that later).

Everything I did was focused on video and music and making more and more visual videos to stand out. Whenever I went to see a band, I would daydream about how the video would look and what I could create and I'd get really excited. I didn't play an instrument myself, but I could see the music. Sometimes I would write the idea down and not send it to the band, but other times I would approach the band after a gig to see if they needed a clip.

My dad had a record store when I was growing up, and the videos and music really went hand in hand. I became obsessed with music videos. I watched a program called *rage* on the ABC, the government TV station in Australia. It was a music video show that ran all night long, and it was a dream for someone like me. I would watch it for as long as my eyes would stay open. I studied every video and every idea, watching shots, noting techniques, and writing down ideas.

In year twelve at school, I chose media studies as one of my major subjects. Back then, there were only three students in the class. It was seen as one of those subjects you do to muck around at school, but I embraced the subject completely. I think I was the only one who was serious about wanting to work in the industry. When I think back, I can't believe how wise and how in tune with my choices I was. I didn't care what other people thought or how many others were doing things. I was focused on where I had to go.

I loved how there were only three of us in that class. It meant I could do more and get more help. How times have changed! Media classes today are completely full of people.

For my final project in year twelve, I created my first-ever music video. I had permission to film in the old Adelaide jail and I had my dad mime an Iggy Pop song called "Isolation." I filmed it all on VHS, and that was when I came across my first technical challenge!

When I went to edit my video, I saw that there was tape damage all through the video, right across the middle. I couldn't believe it, after all my hard work! I couldn't do anything about it. I was devastated that after all the planning and filming, my video was ruined. I think this is where my perfectionism bug started to show. I still received high grades, though. On my teacher's report, he wrote that I was the best student he had taught in thirteen years of teaching. I'll never forget that, despite the technical glitch.

Always remember that even the most experienced people have things that come up during the video-making process. It doesn't mean you're bad at it. It's just a part of life, and happens to *every* professional and amateur I know.

Media Studies

The next step in my path was figuring out where to study. I remember I had this feeling that university wasn't for me. It seemed like a waste of time unless I could go to a film school. I didn't see the point, but went ahead and applied to and was accepted by a local university to do a communications degree, which was a general media studies program. I wasn't excited like most people were about going to Uni. My heart wasn't in it. I wanted a job in the media industry. I thought about it and realized that I could be ahead of the rest of the people still studying if I could get a job sooner.

Then something happened on the day before I had to make the decision about whether or not to attend uni: An opportunity at a media school that I hadn't even known about came to my attention. It was called MAPS (Media and Photography School). I called straight away and got an interview for the one-year film, video, design, and photography program. I remember asking the teacher I talked with what percent of students found employment after doing the program. He said over 50 percent. I decided that by doing this course and skipping university I would get into the industry sooner rather than later... and it worked!

Thinking about it now, I'm grateful for my strong intuition back then, and that I was smart enough to listen to it. If I'd waited, I'd only be competing with hundreds more people for jobs.

When I was only three months into my one-year program at MAPS, I landed a freelance job at Channel 10 TV in Adelaide. Pretty amazing and so exciting! My dreams were happening exactly like I had hoped they would.

First Job in TV

The story of how I got the job at Channel 10 is another

example of how clear it was that this was the path I was being called to. As a part of my MAPS program, we got to do a guided tour of the Channel 10 studio. I was sitting by the security desk at Channel 10, waiting for my tour guide to arrive, when I overheard someone talking to the security guard, saying they needed someone for an animation job for a kid's show called *Mulligrubs*.

I didn't know a thing about animation. It was a weird moment because this excited feeling grew inside my stomach and this little voice inside me said, "Go on! Yell out. Say something! Now is your chance!"

So I did. I yelled out to the man talking and said, "I'll do it." We talked, and he gave me his number and said to call him later and he would run through the job with me. I couldn't believe how it had happened. I was beside myself with excitement. I could hardly focus on the rest of the tour.

What was also weird was that I had *never* been one to speak out before then. I was introverted and normally as quiet as a mouse with people I didn't know. But something inside had told me to do it.

So, that was the beginning. I went to Channel 10 for a tour and came out with a well-paid freelance job where I could choose my own hours. The job was only for three months, but then I applied for a full-time job in the videotape department, putting commercials to air. I wanted to work from the ground up so I could get an understanding of every facet of the industry. In my eyes, that would make me a better director.

In the videotape department at Channel 10, I worked with large machines, putting 24 commercials per shift to air manually during advert breaks. My shifts would range from eight to twelve hours, sometimes more. For a year and a half, I was on 4 a.m. starts that ran through until 1 p.m. Not fun for a girl who loved going out and staying up late. Terrible for my social life and my sleeping patterns. It felt like mopping floors would have been a better job. The room where I worked was dark, cold, and had no windows. It was loud. The industrial noise of the machines was constant. The toxic chemicals I had to use when cleaning machines started to eat away at my skin.

I felt like a fish out of water and found it hard to get my head around the job. There were lots of things I had to do very fast and focused, and if I made an error and put a commercial to air that was wrong, I'd cost the station thousands of dollars. I used to do that quite often. I just wasn't suited to that particular job. Each day I would look for an opportunity to get out of there and find an opening somewhere else. But I look back and know that it taught me about focus and attention to detail.

The good thing was that I did learn the industry from the bottom up. In that job, I learned some basics about editing, videos, advertising, and people. But I think it was there that my confidence started on a downward spiral. I often talk about that experience with older directors and people in the movie industry and they share similar experiences. We all still have nightmares of the old ACR machines failing and the TV station going to black on air, causing millions of people to change the channel. If that was your fault, it was a *huge deal!*

When the Gulf War broke out, we worked even longer hours, and I saw war images 24/7 because I had to watch what was airing in order to be able to time the commercials right. It was haunting listening to the POWs speak and seeing death and destruction all the time. I remember having nightmares and feeling scared about the world. Being constantly surrounded by bad news had a negative effect on me. I started to fear everything. I hardly watch TV at all now, and I don't watch the news. To me, news is fear-mongering and hyper-focusing on the negative. I hope we can redefine "news" to include the fun, and the inspirational.

People are starting to wake up about not wanting to see bad news all the time. People want to be inspired. Look at TED talks and how popular they are. Imagine if we had good news stories on, inspirational stories with no doom and gloom. People want to see possibility in the world instead of fear. They want to be inspired about what's possible and not be scared to get on a plane or get in a car or travel to a foreign land. When I switched off all negative news, it made a massive shift in my thinking. People have so much subconscious fear today because of being brainwashed by the media.

* * *

Moving Upstairs

After a long two years of putting commercials to air, I finally escaped from the dungeon, as I like to call it, and I moved upstairs. I'd taken to sitting with the graphic designers during my breaks, hoping to hear about a job coming up, which I finally did. The design department was getting a new machine and, in my new job, I was going to learn how to use it and integrate it. It was like the job was created just for me.

I worked at Channel 10 in Adelaide for seven years, working in all facets of the media, and finally ended up directing promos and doing motion design. I loved directing. I got so excited about the whole process, from coming up with the concept right through to filming and editing. It was like I was on a high; the adrenalin was amazing. It was creative work and I had to shake myself when I thought about how I was being paid to do it. How lucky was I?

I'm really grateful that design was one of the things that fascinated me. The design of your videos will make them stand out. The design is in the style, the brand, the essence of who you are. We'll talk more about that later.

In the design department at Channel 10, I was terrible at first. Not that I knew I was terrible! I thought I was okay until I started opening my eyes to the designs around me. One day, I was even told how bad I was, but I still really couldn't see it. I was told I'd be sent back down to the dungeon if I didn't lift my game and start making better graphics and designs! Those comments back then were just what I needed to hear. Sometimes it takes the truth to set you free, that's for sure.

I started working all night and reading books, copying designs, and learning whatever I could so I wouldn't have to go back down to the adverts videotape department.

It was around that time that I started feeling the pressure of being in a male-dominated industry. I loved working with men, but anytime there were opportunities for promotion, a guy would be chosen over me. When I look back, it definitely was a bit of a boys' club.

You needed a thick skin in those days of working in TV. It was fun too, don't get me wrong. I created strong bonds with people working here, and they still feel like family. Because of the strange, long hours, you develop amazing connections for life.

I also think that having so much time on my own when I was working in that atmosphere wasn't good for me. I was alone with my thoughts for too long. The self-doubt would come in, and I would talk down to myself all day long. I can only see this now, in hindsight, and I only realize now that I was the creator of my reality.

That's when my whole mindset started to change for the worse. It's true that you start being like those you spend the most time with, and that's what happened. I never felt good enough, and in the rare times when I almost did, someone was there to cut me back down.

The Boys' Club

There was definitely a boys' club in the media industry when I first started. It has evened out by now. I think ego mixed with fame affected a lot of people in the media. There were massive egos everywhere. In those days, having a TV job was like having rockstar status. When you said you worked in TV, people would instantly be interested in what you had to say.

I don't want to go on about the boys' club too much, because I know women can be just as bad. What I'm telling you was my experience.

There was one celebrity who stood out. He was one of the most sexist people I had to deal with on a daily basis at Channel 10. He would say crude comments to me all the time, like, "Your ass is too big for that chair, isn't it?"

If I yawned, he would say, "Yes, but no thanks." He was a dirty old man with a big ego. I put in a formal complaint and was asked by management to withdraw it because of who he was. I decided I'd give him one more chance. I knew it would only be a matter of time before it happened again. I heard the way he spoke to other people in the newsroom. The ego that man had was the biggest I've ever witnessed. I couldn't believe what I was hearing on some days. What surprised me the most was what he got away with. No one had the courage to stand up to him because of who he was.

Sure enough, after a while, he said something again and this time pushed me too far. He called me a "f**cking slut" because the fax machine didn't work. What was even more disturbing was the fact no one stepped up to do anything about it. I got a couple of side glances from a couple of people and I shrank in my chair. I was as red as a beetroot and didn't know what to say back to him. There were a lot of things I *wanted* to say, but I was embarrassed and didn't know how he would react. How dare someone speak to me like that! So, this time, I went to the station manager and told him what had happened. I wasn't going to be ignored again. The next day the celebrity with the big ego came straight to me and was obnoxious because he'd found out that I'd stood up to him.

Over the next few days, things went a little quiet, and all of a sudden the celebrity resigned. I don't know the exact details of what happened.

If you've ever watched the show *The Newsroom,* you have a pretty good idea of how it really is in a newsroom situation. Where I worked was a lot like that. The man with the big ego went to another TV station and has now retired from the media. I know my incident wasn't an isolated one. I'm reluctant to talk about it, even now. I'm a different person now than I was back then, but it's important to share this with you because I know how much this kind of thing happens in the work place.

I'm very proud of how I handled it, especially considering how hard it was at the time to speak up and despite having no support from anyone around me for a long time. No one deserves to be treated that way. I followed my instincts. I'm sharing this with you in the hope that if something like this happens to you, you stick up for yourself. If you know in your heart that it's wrong, do something about it.

For the most part, I loved working with men. Most of my best friends were men. However, in TV I found there to be some groups of men who, when they were together, were outspoken and obnoxious. I seemed to attract more and more of those types of men until it got to the point where I had a breakdown.

On to Sydney

After seven years, I'd gone as far as I could in Adelaide, so I applied for a transfer to Channel 10 in Sydney. I knew that by moving to the biggest city in Australia I was more likely to get the work I wanted. I could go after my dream of being the music clip director I was born to be. I got the job and went to Sydney on my own. I was a young girl in a big city.

I started in the motion design department and stayed there for a few years and I grew so much. It was in Sydney that I started my first side business, called Raw Vision Productions, so I could direct my own music videos. I was in my 20s and was directing some of the biggest names in Australia at that time. I directed videos for Vanessa Amorossi, Adam Harvey, Tina Cousins, John Williamson, Becky Cole, Travis, and Brad Cole. I directed about 40 music videos during that period.

I worked non-stop, learning and creating. Because I didn't really know many people in Sydney, I was able to focus on perfecting my craft. I was nominated for best music video award at the Golden Guitar Awards in 2004. It was a great year, as I was also nominated for best director by the Country Music Association. Back then, I was terrified of winning because I didn't want to have to get up in front of all those people to accept an award! I was so scared of everything, which is quite amazing to me now.

I loved the whole process of making music videos and couldn't believe that I got to create videos out of my imagination for people to use to promote themselves. I remember one day on a set when I was directing "Shine" for Vanessa Amorossi. I took a moment to be present. I was so grateful for the experience. I truly loved what I was doing. I loved the collaboration, I loved the creativity, and I even loved the stress at the end when I delivered the product and waited for reactions. That was a big adrenalin rush.

BETTER VIDEOS

. . .

Out of Alignment

I created music videos for over ten years under my own banner, while still working full time in TV. For a few of those years, I worked at a different TV station, where I stayed until being made redundant in 2004. The redundancy was a shock to my system – I wasn't expecting it at all. Everyone spoke about it being a possibility, but no one thought it would actually happen. When it did happen, it was like my identity had been taken away, because everything I knew was about TV. I thought I had made it! Then there was that moment when I was handed the envelope in the office. I remember thinking being laid off was voluntary and saying, "Oh no, that's okay, I've decided I'll stay."

When I was told that I had no choice, I was in complete shock. The tears welled up in my eyes and I thought, "Don't cry, don't cry." I'd been working full-time and doing my music video business on the side. Without my job, I didn't know who I was.

That was also a weird time because technology was going through massive changes, and if I didn't stay ahead of them, I was going to be left behind. I did freelance work for a while in addition to my music videos, but I always felt like I was lagging behind with knowing what I could do with the new equipment, because I hadn't had the training. I wasn't sure what my next steps should be.

After my layoff, I went into a deep depression. I was also diagnosed with narcolepsy. Narcolepsy is a chronic brain disorder that involves poor control of sleep-wake cycles. People with narcolepsy experience periods of extreme daytime sleepiness and sudden, irresistible bouts of sleep that can strike at any time. These "sleep attacks" usually last a few seconds to several minutes.

Narcolepsy can greatly affect daily activities. People with narcolepsy may unwillingly fall asleep while at work or at school, when having a conversation, playing a game, eating a meal, or, most dangerously, when driving or operating other types of machinery. Luckily, my narcolepsy is manageable now, and I only really require one nap a day. (That's another great thing about creating your own business – you can nap when you like!)

In addition to daytime sleepiness, one of the major symptoms I have is cataplexy, which is a sudden loss of voluntary muscle tone while awake that makes me go limp or be unable to move. Although cataplexy can occur spontaneously, it's more often triggered by sudden, strong emotions, such as fear, anger, stress, excitement, or humor. Laughter is the most frustrating thing about having cataplexy. When I was diagnosed, I was put on medication to dull down my senses and keep me awake. My emotions were now more controlled, so I wouldn't collapse when I laughed. Weird, huh? Most people say laughter is the best medicine.

All of that knocked the confidence out of me. It was really hard to keep working, because I wanted to sleep all the time. I found focusing really difficult – especially after the redundancy, when I was unsure of who I was. The medication I was on during that time was terrible and dulled my emotions.

I became even more of a workaholic. It wasn't healthy. I stopped eating and I just worked. It wasn't healthy working, either. It was like I was on speed or had drunk ten coffees. I had the ability to work longer, because of the medication I was on, and I withdrew, working on creative projects to keep my mind off the reality of my situation. At the time I was diagnosed, a few other people in the department where I was freelancing were also quite sick with different things. I always wondered if that had anything to do with working under a giant satellite dish and around so many electrical devices.

At the time, I couldn't see the pattern that was starting to develop. Because I was feeling isolated at home and was working non-stop, my fiancé, Michael, and I decided it would be good for me to move to a big studio in Sydney, so I could be around more people. Then I could be seen and feel like I was part of a community again.

I was accepted as a studio's local director specializing in music videos and commercials that were designer-based. The studio was in a great location and I ended up leasing a space from them for my own business. I shared the office space, splitting it with another business. I hoped that it would be a great alliance that would lead to collaboration, because I craved working within a community again and the feeling of being valued.

That was when the Girl Director name was born, because I wanted to stand out and I wanted people to know that I was a girl and I was a director. It made perfect sense to me, especially in a male-dominated field. I created a virtual character as my logo to help my brand stand out. With many men being producers in the industry, I also thought that having a sexy-looking logo would be great marketing. I had lost my confidence and thought that if I had a character to help me get out there and market my business, I'd have an edge over a lot of people. And I did.

I was in that production office for about two years, and that was the hardest time in my career, for sure, because I was doing what I thought I *should* do and not what my heart was telling me to do. I really had no business skills – but there's nothing like having a business of your own when you want to learn what you're good at and what you aren't!

I'm grateful for that time, because it taught me that I needed better business, sales, and marketing skills. Without them, how could I survive? For example, I was terrified of the phone. I bent over backward to help clients, but then when they wouldn't pay me I wasn't firm enough with my boundaries and systems. I would over-promise. And when the computer was playing up, I started to miss things and blow deadlines, which stressed me out even more.

I was on a downward spiral, aggravated by the medication I was on. In spite of the move to the bigger studio, I felt more and more disconnected and often focused on the wrong things. Even so, my creativity during that time was amazing, and I created some of the best work I've ever done, because my attention to design and detail was what I was mostly focusing on. I came to realize that when you work for yourself, your biggest competitor *is* yourself. I used to beat myself up, telling myself that I wasn't as good as other people, and that would drive me to do even more. One day, I finally realized how good I actually was and that I'd become my own worst enemy by competing with myself.

There were some great, supportive people in the building where I worked; one of my best friends was there. However, there were also some assholes – that is truly the only way to describe them. I know I attracted them; I can see now that I was a magnet for people who treated me terribly. Mainly, it was because I didn't value myself. I attracted clients who wouldn't pay on time or didn't value my effort, even though they loved the videos I made. The more I gave, the more they took. I started to suffer from serious self-doubt. My confidence was at an all-time low.

Michael was working full-time in the corporate world. He was supporting us as best he could, but we weren't making the money we wanted to be making. I really wanted Michael to come on board with me. I knew that, together, we would be amazing team, but we couldn't give up the money from his day job. I honestly didn't know what I was doing wrong then, but when I look back, I can see that I had so many fears going on.

Michael and I fought more and more, and my medication was changing my personality. I was taking high doses of the narcolepsy medication every day to stay awake, and I was obsessed with trying to make everything work. I couldn't see a way forward.

I really wish I'd had a mentor then, someone to work with who could have helped me move forward more easily, someone to talk with on a regular basis who could have guided me and told me the things that were missing.

The Confidence Equation

Looking back now, I can see that not believing in myself was my biggest problem. Money was tight, my energy was low, and I attracted the worst clients because of it – clients who didn't value my work and didn't view me in the way I thought they should. I thought if I gave more it would help me. That plan backfired.

Video started to represent everything I didn't like: ego, money, and bullies. Those things weren't anything like the person I was and wanted to be. I started to see the greedy, ugly side of video. The reason I'd started in the video industry in the first place was to be creative, to make a difference in the world and open people's minds to a new way of thinking. But all video was doing was creating stress for me. I was unhappy, had no confidence left, and felt I had nowhere to turn.

All the things I didn't like about the video industry were so bad at the big studio that I moved to a different office.

That was when I completely lost it and had a nervous breakdown, because I moved out of the smoke and into the fire. My new office was the nastiest place I have ever come across, though I didn't realize it until I was there. There was corruption there like nowhere else I had experienced. I was told lies and stories – and at first I believed them. I always took people at face value and if they told me something, I believed them. I always saw the good in people and couldn't imagine that there were such selfish people out there with so little respect for other people.

The office cleaner alarmed me one day when she asked why there had been people in my office on a day when I had been out filming. She said they'd been at my computer. I found out that the people who owned the space were using the building's master key to go into my office and read my emails. I checked my computer's backlog and found out there had been someone there. I should have confronted them about the situation then, but instead I got stuck trying to work out why they would do that. I felt paralyzed and was obsessed with wanting to know *why*. It didn't make any sense to me that it was happening. Why would someone do that unless they were trying to learn our IP address and take advantage of it? They were also able to see my incoming emails, as they went through a joint server. Things becoming so bad that I spoke to a lawyer. Things started to get worse after I heard back from my lawyer.

The people in the building where my new office was located had hired my staff behind my back, and they never paid me for the four TV commercials my business delivered, even though they were already airing them on television. All of that happened during a six-month period that felt like years.

One day, my lawyer told me to get out of the building as soon as possible because he'd found out that the people we were dealing with were very corrupt. They had an advertising agency that worked mainly with the Mafia. They could take all of our gear and lock us out of the building.

So, at midnight, we packed up the office and left. I was scared, burned out, tired, and not sure what to do anymore. I honestly didn't know what the hell had happened and, most importantly, I still didn't know why.

I was a wreck. I cried all the time and didn't want anything to do with video anymore. But I didn't know anything else to do, so I felt very lost. I needed to rest and figure out what I was going to do. I ended up going home to Adelaide to spend time away from Sydney, be with family, and get clarity again.

I took time off, rested, and stopped taking the medication so I could get my sleeping pattern back to normal. Then I saw the problem: I had lost my passion for video. I wasn't connected anymore to my big picture of why video was important to me. I had done some branding work with the Girl Director name, but I wasn't really living the Girl Director life. I was hiding behind the persona. The girl who impressed her year twelve media studies teacher in high school was gone, and in her place was some kind of sad robot.

By the time I went back to work in Sydney and picked up the Girl Director brand again, things were different. I was different. I said goodbye to clients who didn't respect my work and I said goodbye to work that wasn't in line with my purpose. I was clear about my big picture, aligned with my brand, and living and working from my Video Super Power: my special skills in video.

It took a while, but over the next few years Michael quit his job and came to work with me, and together, with the help of a couple of great mentors, we took Girl Director online and turned it into a business model that is fun, on our terms, and lucrative. And I was right, by the way. Michael and

I do make a great team! I'll tell you more about him later. I was amazed that we could turn things around from not being paid properly to having clients respecting us and paying us well to help them.

There's a key take-away lessons here: *Find the right clients*, the ones you love and who respect you.

* * *

What's Blocking Your Success with Video?

I want to share some insights with you about what might be blocking *your* success, because I want you to know that I get it. It took having a nervous breakdown and making all the mistakes in the world for me to get it, but I'm here right now sharing my mistakes with you so that you can learn from them.

When you don't believe in yourself, you attract the wrong clients. When you make videos for everyone else that aren't aligned with who you are and that don't move you, they won't work. Videos are fun and creative, and you can make a massive difference with your clients and in the world – *when you are aligned*.

I don't want you to go through the things I went through to learn the secrets of making great videos. I want you to follow my guidance in this book and embrace your Video Super Power to reach, engage with, and help those you were born to help. There's a massive shift happening in the world right now as more and more women step up to use video to be leaders and to communicate powerful stories. They're helping to bridge gaps and open minds to new possibilities. It's such an exciting time right now to be involved with video!

The one thing I've learned for sure on my journey is that you have to get real. Get real about your strengths and your weaknesses. Get real about what you love and hate. Get real about what works for you and what doesn't. Yes, there are camera techniques and lighting styles you can learn about that will help you make great videos – but the most important ingredient is *you being in alignment with your passion*. No video technique will fix it if you're out of alignment. Alignment is what will make your videos stand out to the right people *for you*.

How do you feel about being on camera? If your time in front of the camera doesn't flow easily, it's because of one or more of these reasons: fear of what others will think, worry about the video not being perfect enough, or not feeling passionate about the subject you're talking about. Are you connecting with what you're saying? Maybe it's only what you think you should say rather than what your heart is telling you to say.

When you're living your passion, nothing will stop you from making the difference you want to be making. People see beyond looks. They see beyond the technical aspects. They see and know when your video is truly from the heart. The way to conquer this fear is to step in, "feel the fear, and do it anyway".

THE GIRL DIRECTOR SOLUTION FRAMEWORK

Plan. Produce. Promote.

I'm so excited that you're here and ready to embrace video. You're going to love it. I've spent over twenty years and many thousands of dollars to learn the stuff I'm about to share with you. This book will save you time and money so you can start implementing sooner and with ease.

I mentioned Michael, my life partner and business partner, in the previous chapter. I want to introduce him properly now, because he's the co-director of Girl Director and has some very important roles. He's my rock and looks after me very well – I'm lucky. Michael is the details man and I'm the big-picture person. I do the branding, content, mentoring, and coaching, while he runs our marketing campaigns, handles the editing, works with the lights and sound during video shoots, wears the producer hat regarding budgets, and oversees the crew and staff. I feel very grateful that we have different skills that allow us to work so well together. This is what I've always wanted: someone to work with side by side. Without his support, I wouldn't be here writing this book.

I'm not saying you can't make great videos on your own, because you can. Most of our clients do, and I did for years. But I got to the point where I wanted a life partner I could grow with and share a life with. We live where we want to and we work together on things that are important to us. It's interesting to see that when someone works with us as a client, they also see what's available to them in a relationship and what is possible for their life. This type of close, mutually beneficial collaboration is possible for your life, too.

You're going to learn so much from this book. As you read through, identify *three new ways* you can grow your business using video. This is something I always do when I go to an event and feel overwhelmed by all of the new information coming at me. Picking three things gives you an intention. I do something similar with the videos I produce: I always aim to *really love* at least ten seconds of every video I create. Being selective and looking for those three key things you can add to your business or your life will take the pressure off having to remember everything. I would *love* to hear what you choose!

* * *

A word on perfection from a recovering perfectionist before we begin: The important thing is to keep moving. When you start this process, you may not like the video you create, but the important thing is to keep going. Think of how many videos you've seen that were so compelling you couldn't keep your eyes off the person you were watching, even though the video quality was terrible.

Many people think making a video is only about getting the right camera, lights, and microphone, but there are some very important foundational things to get right first. You can easily pick up the technical stuff by coming to one of our events or checking out some of the cool video-techy lessons we've included as links at the end of this book. But don't get stuck on the technical stuff. Or, if you do, contact us, because we're looking at doing some virtual techy how-to classes. You never know what cool things we'll think up in order to help you!

The most important steps for you to learn are in this book. If you skip one of these steps, I promise you it will show up negatively in your results and to the people you want to connect to. Generally, if your marketing isn't working or your videos aren't getting the results you want, it always comes back to your answers to these questions:

1. Do you get great results with the product or service you're marketing?
2. Are you really passionate about the thing you're marketing?
3. Is your message too complicated?
4. Is there a need out there in the marketplace for what you have?

This book will help you answer these questions. I'll be introducing you to our Girl Director process, which is based on our three P's: Plan, Produce, and Promote. These are the foundational steps for making and creating better videos, videos that help you stand out and attract the clients you were born to help.

You're reading this because you want to make a difference in the world, as well as look great in your videos and attract more clients. Keep that thought in mind as you go through this book, because when you start focusing on your clients' needs instead of all the other things, that's when the big shift happens. Don't overcomplicate things. It's doing the simple but powerful things – the ones that are often staring right at you – that will get you the biggest results.

* * *

In the introduction, I shared my story of the good, the bad, and the ugly in my video career to inspire you into action and show you that, no matter what happened, those tests were there to push me to the next level, every single time.

In the next couple of chapters, I'll go into more detail about types of videos, common problems, and how to solve them. In Chapter 3, coming up, you'll learn about your own Video Super Power. In Chapter 4, you're going to learn about why it's important to know your audience, and you'll start to learn how to write your perfect script. You'll also learn about setting an intention and creating a start, a middle, and an end to your video, as well as getting clear about how you want to leave your audience once they've watched your video.

In Chapter 5, I'll go through the different types of videos for marketing and what they're used for, to give you an overall understanding so that you can pick one and start there.

Chapters 6 through 8 get into creating clients, avoiding things that can sabotage success, and being a ROCKSTAR.

In Chapter 9, we get into the fun of filming and I get a little techy to help you with gear and tell you the must-haves for making better videos.

Chapter 10 is about your legacy and how what you put out into the world creates a ripple effect with every video you make and share.

At the end of the book are links to bonus tools to help you even more with getting started.

As you read through the book, have paper and pen next to

you so you can take lots of notes. And remember to take away three things to implement. Have fun!

Girl Director Secret Technique

The number one trick for making better videos is being confident on camera. Quiet down the mind chatter so that you can communicate your message in the most powerful way. Once this aspect shifts, other things in your life will also shift. Let's start at the very beginning, with you getting used to seeing yourself on screen. For help with this, check out our FREE camera confidence course at https://www.youtube.com/girldirectorTV

THE BIG PICTURE

Always see people bigger than they see themselves and then watch them magically step into that place.

This chapter is about developing and stretching into your own bigger picture, aligning with your passion, and getting clear on the vision of where you see yourself going, so you can start to stretch into that place where you want to be. Your life is your movie screen, so if you don't like what's playing, it's time to change the vision in your mind.

Making videos is exactly the same. You'll start to see the world very differently as you read this book. You'll begin noticing locations to film your videos, you'll have more confidence, and you'll know exactly what video can do for you and your business. You may even tap into an idea that you feel drawn to use to make an even bigger difference in the world, like creating a documentary.

Video is a passion that makes my heart sing – specifically, music videos, motion design, and making a difference. I *love* opening up new ways of thinking for people. I *love* finding unique stories and new ways of looking at the world in order to open new conversations. I *love* helping people make videos and saving them thousands of dollars in production costs. I *love* watching confidence build in people when they embrace video. I also *love* watching women who have been invisible for so much of their lives take flight and blossom in big ways.

When you step into the shoes of being a director, you also become a better leader and a better communicator through your use of images and emotion.

Video becomes so much more fun when you're fully plugged in to your passion. When you're in tune with what you *love* to create, you'll be more productive. You'll move mountains to get things done and you'll be excited to create your own video content.

Your Video Super Power

I want you to think about the following statements and rate them on a scale of one to ten, where one is "*NO, THAT'S NOT ME,*" and ten is "*YES, THAT'S TOTALLY ME!* ". Don't think about your answers for too long. Write down the first number on the scale that comes to mind. Developing this awareness is a great first step.

1. **The Actor:** I love being in front of the camera, as I have great charisma that draws others in.
2. **The Comedian:** I love comedy and love being wacky and funny in front of the camera.
3. **The Reality TV Star:** I love reality TV shows and would love to have cameras set up all over my house as a way to inspire others.
4. **The Interviewer:** I love to interview people and

secretly wish I was Oprah Winfrey, with my own show.
5. **The Journalist:** I love getting into the thick of things and would love to be a journalist uncovering the truth. I want to expand global consciousness.
6. **The Documentary Maker**: I love exploring the world and nature and would love to make documentaries like David Attenborough.
7. **The Director**: I love being behind the scenes, coming up with the ideas, and making it happen. I am good at delegating tasks. I want to run a video agency
8. **The Drama Director:** I love drama and making up stories, and want to create my own dramatic TV series or movie.
9. **The Music Video Director:** I love music and music videos and want to use them to communicate my message.
10. **The Animation Director:** I love animation and special effects and would love to have a cartoon character that saves the world while teaching at the same time.

Most people have more than one interest when it comes to making videos, so once you have your set of ten scores, list the top two or three and put them together to create a composite description of what you love. Be creative with it. Use your imagination to see what you can come up with here by combining different ways you're attracted to working with video. The result is your **Video Super Power**! This is the way of working that inspires you and will drive you toward your goal. To give you an idea, my Video Super Powers are working with motion design, documentaries, and opening up new ways of thinking and looking at the world. There is no right or wrong here. This is all about honing in on the thing that will inspire you to create videos you're passionate about.

Now it's time to start making videos that make the most of your Video Super Power!

If you're still not clear about which direction to go, here's a little hint about where to find your passion: Think about the last time you were watching TV or watching a video on the Internet and saw something that really upset you or really inspired you. Remember how you wanted to drop everything to help that person, animal, or situation? How it made you so angry or so inspired that you wanted to do something right then to help? When you felt those emotions, whatever you were watching is very close to the thing you're passionate about, and that includes the type of video it was.

So, what was it?

Whatever it was, *that* is what you can start to make a video about, and *that* is what is giving you clues about your Video Super Power. When you're aligned with what lights you up, you attract amazing things into your life.

*** * ***

Whenever I want something to show up in my life, I always ask questions. I ask myself, "*What will it take* for an idea to show up in my life that inspires me to action?" and "*What will it take* for me to find something I'm passionate about?" and "*What would it take* for a new client to show up this week?" Try asking yourself questions like these or whatever types of questions have meaning for you.

Don't ask yourself negative questions like, "*Why can't I* think of something that would be great and life-changing?" or "*Why don't I* have clients?" Instead, ask, "*What would it take* for me to meet more clients?" By reframing your questions to yourself as positive, the answers come. You'll see.

BETTER VIDEOS

To help you understand what I mean, let me share a story about asking questions.

After my nervous breakdown, I didn't want to do the same kind of work again, so I did some non-video freelance work for a while, which was great. It was just what I needed to do to pay the bills and take a break. During that time, I kept asking myself questions like the ones I mentioned above. I did that every day until one day, when I was in the shower, I had an idea about an elephant.

All of a sudden, I had a weird thought. I wondered, "What if I could work with an elephant and teach the elephant how to use the camera? What if I could build a friendship with the elephant and help the elephant communicate? What if the elephant was communicating with me?" This may sound freaky and, believe me, I thought so at the time. The weirdest part was that I didn't (yet) have a passion for elephants. I didn't know anything about them. I started wondering where that idea had come from.

All the ideas you have aren't necessarily yours. When I started to learn more about animal communication, I couldn't believe that all the ideas I'd had weren't only mine. You may think the ideas you have are yours, but they're just out there. And there are loads of them. It's strange that when a big movie is released, there's often another one released at the same time on the same subject. Ideas are out there waiting for our consciousness to receive them.

I got out of the shower and was so excited that this idea about an elephant had ignited my passion again. It ticked all the boxes for me: it was an adventure, it was helpful, it was about animals, and it involved using all of my video skills. I kept asking myself those open questions and more answers came to me. That's how my documentary, *Through Elephant Eyes*, was born. The idea was about making a difference to an animal and also opening up the minds of others. It was also about the possibility of a new way of thinking, using video and using all the things I'm passionate about.

I thought Michael would think I was crazy. When I raced out of the shower to tell him, though, he was so supportive. He loved it. He said, "What a great idea. Why don't you go and do it?"

So that was it. I went to Thailand – just me, my camera, and a microphone. It didn't matter that I didn't have the budget, or that I was scared to be on camera, or that I would be traveling overseas on my own for the first time, or that I would be going off my narcolepsy medication for the first time, or that it was dangerous. Something about the idea had moved me so much that I *had* to do it. This was a big lesson the elephants taught me: that when the cause is bigger than yourself or about something besides yourself, you don't care about being on camera. You find ways to make it work.

At the beginning of that trip, my camera fear was crippling, though. That was one thing I was scared of more than anything else. Weird, huh? Even though I'd tried really hard to get in front of the camera before, I always froze up. I'd make weird faces. Every single time I was on camera, I didn't like the person looking back. I didn't feel good enough, thin enough, or feel like my hair was long enough. I thought I should look or sound better and I wondered, "What do I know?" and "Who would listen to me?" This kind of thinking is crippling.

If this sounds like you, I completely understand. This self-sabotaging self-talk wasn't good for me and isn't good for you either. You *are* enough. You *are* perfect. There are people who *do* want to listen to what you say.

Please reach out if this is you. I am so passionate about helping women to become *visible*, especially those who are great at what they do yet aren't sure about how to be on camera – because that was me.

BETTER VIDEOS

Since I knew the elephants couldn't speak, I was going to be their voice. So I kept telling myself to get over it and snap out of it. My fear of being on camera didn't go away easily, not until I designed some exercises to help.

If you're wondering how I found a way to get over my camera fear, I'll share a great exercise with you now. Draw three columns on a sheet of paper and think for a minute of three people you love on screen. In the first column, write down their names. They could be anyone you find inspiring and love to watch – personalities, musicians, TV stars. Anyone you're really drawn to.

Now that you have these people in your mind, in the second column write down the traits you like about each person. That could be their looks, personality, sense of humor, or the way they present themselves. There are no right or wrong answers here.

In the third column, write down all the traits you share with these people.

Yes. Cool, huh? What have you noticed? Do you see that you share lots of the same traits? You look to and like people who share similar traits as you.

Now think about what you need to do on camera to start taking on and channeling some of those traits.

I did this exercise before going to Thailand and it really helped me when I was doing interviews or anything in front of the camera. I would think of one of the people I'd put on my list, so I wouldn't be thinking about myself. For example, one of the people on my list was the documentarian Louis Theroux. I would have him in mind as I talked to interviewees. The way he connects so innocently with people is a brilliant way of drawing people out to tell their stories. Depending on what I was doing, I would think of different people from my list and that would elicit other ways of being on camera. Doing this is a way to anchor yourself to your way of being on camera.

* * *

So, the time finally came when I was off to Thailand. I was scared. At times, I wondered why on earth this idea had me so driven that I would travel to an unknown country to work with an animal I knew nothing about. Michael drove me to the airport, and when I was at the check-in counter the woman upgraded me to business class for *free*. She said, "Oh, I just upgraded you to business class." I was in shock. Nothing like that had ever happened to me before. I took it as a sign that I was on my path and things would be okay.

I traveled around Thailand for three months interviewing people about elephants. Weirdly enough, the very first elephant I met, who was named Peter, had just done a Samsung advert for TV and he'd used a phone to take photographs. How freaky was that? After all that time wondering about an elephant being able to take photos, the first one I happened to meet had recently done just that. Hmm. Coincidence? Perhaps. Actually, elephants have 20,000 muscles in their trunks, so they can use a touch pad better than we can!

I interviewed all kinds of people and I followed my instincts. I wasn't sure where to go, so I'd wait until something felt right and then move in that direction. I witnessed sad things and inspirational things. I wanted to film even more than I did, but without the proper passes and government approvals, I hit a few dead ends.

For two years after I got back from Thailand, I left the documentary alone. It didn't feel like the right time to finish it. The subject matter was a little out there, but now I feel like the world is ready for it. It will open up new ways of thinking.

Sometimes documentaries take time to make, depending on the story and the market. That's why you want to make something you're passionate about – because it can take longer than you expect.

As I mentioned, my Video Super Powers are directing with motion design, documentaries, and opening up new ways of thinking and looking at the world. I *love* those things! Can you see how that one idea about the elephants was so charged for me that I had to do it, no matter what? I didn't have the money, I didn't have all the gear I'd need, and, hell, I didn't even know if what I was doing was real rather than just a dream. What I did know was that if I followed my passion, things would evolve and change.

Going to Thailand to work with the elephants is why I'm here right now talking to you. My crippling fear of being on camera had stopped me from making as big a difference as I'd wanted to, but while I was in Thailand, so many people told me stories that were wanting to be shared with the world. I could see amazing documentaries everywhere. That got me thinking that when I got home, I could turn the Girl Director brand into an iconic and visionary company that mentors women and teaches them to embrace video so that they, too, can make a difference. I could help them grow their confidence and learn video that so they could communicate to more people. There are too many stories for just me alone to tell!

The longer I do this work, the more I notice amazing women who are hidden away, invisible from the world. They're masters at what they do, but they're stuck, and they see technology as a barrier. You are here, reading this book, because you have a deep desire to make a difference and you instinctively know that video is the key to helping yourself and helping the people you want to reach.

At first, I was worried about having competition out there – other people teaching women about video – but there's enough work. There are enough clients out there for everyone. Coming from a place of lack doesn't serve you. If you're worried about what other people think, or if you think there are already too many videos on your subject, you'll never get yours out there. Video is never going away now. It's only going to get bigger and more intense, with live interactive social media channels coming online. Prepare by being more and more connected to what your clients want and by being able to speak live on camera.

By the way, if this is all seems like too much – if you don't feel like you have the confidence, are scared to follow your passion, or feel unable to figure things out on your own – and you'd rather speak to me directly to have help uncovering your Video Super Power, you can email me at iwantvideos@girldirector.com. Sometimes it can be confusing when you're trying to work it out on your own. I want to help you live your passion and create the videos you were born to make. Your video will create change.

A Closer Look at the Kinds of Videos You Can Make

Video is so creative and fun. Now that you know your Video Super Power, let's go deeper into looking at the different types of videos you can make. Notice which types appeal to you as you read through the list below.

Interview show. Perhaps you see yourself as an Oprah Winfrey or Ellen DeGeneres, someone who loves interviewing people and makes a difference at the same time.

Interview shows are great because they tap into other people's client databases, too. (You can check out our YouTube Channel for more information about creating interview shows at youtube.com/girldirectorTV).

Q & A show. Maybe you want to create a question-and-answer show, the way life coach and thought leader Marie Forleo does. Question-and-answer shows are easy to create because you simply find people who want to learn from you and make a video about them each week.

News. Perhaps you like the look of a set with you sitting at the front – alone or with a bunch of other cool people talking about stuff. You can shoot with a green screen and purchase an image to use for the background. Panel shows on TV are often great and interesting. There's no reason you couldn't do this from home or in your own studio space.

Animation. Animation is the term for when something isn't real on the screen. For example, if you're a stylist, you could have clothes that move on the screen as you talk about certain colours working together. You could have an animated character who represents you. This is what I did with the Girl Director logo character.

Documentary. Is David Attenborough more your style? Would you like to travel around doing a lifestyle or cooking show in different places, learning and sharing what you've learned? I *love* expanding my mind by watching documentaries. There are a few different styles of documentary you could make. The important thing is to open up new ideas without your own judgment getting in the way. This was hard for me when making *Through Elephant Eyes*, the documentary that came out of my Thailand trip. I wanted to save the elephants, and before I went to Thailand I felt like I knew the situation, because of all the horrible images I'd seen on the Internet. Well, when I got there, I found out that I didn't really know anything. In order to make a documentary that makes a difference, you have to leave your judgment behind and focus on the job you're there to do. Be open without judgment and see things from other perspectives.

Pictures with a voice. Pictures with text is one of the easiest styles to master. Pictures and photos can say a thousand words, if you chose the images that represent you and your brand. Choose images that create an emotion in the viewer. Always be thinking, "What do I want my audience to feel when they watch this?"

Text on the screen. Typography on a screen that speaks to your ideal client is also very powerful. I've created some great animation with text made from clients' stories combined with powerful music and words. Your video can have the same effect. Your video doesn't always need to be you or someone else in front of the camera. It can be just text.

Cartoon characters. A cartoon character is like the Girl Director character logo image. It can be something as simple as a kids' cartoon series or something more complex, like the animation in the movie *Finding Nemo*. A cartoon character can represent you or what you're talking about.

Stories. Consistency is the key when doing a lifestyle video series. What do people ask you about? What are you good at? Share behind the scenes about what you do. Daily videos around how you work is a great way to build a following. There are many types of businesses this will work for. Service based businesses, coaches, product-based businesses.

Comedy. If you're more of a comedy girl, then go for it! People love to be entertained while they're learning something. If you have a natural flair for making people laugh, now's your chance (We always get great feedback on our blooper videos).

Music videos. Let me guess. As a teenager you were one of those people who used your hairbrush to sing in the mirror, miming to your favourite songs. If music is your thing, making videos that are like music videos may be the way to bring out your Video Super Power. Making music videos is one of my super powers.

Video blogs. Video blogs (also called vlogs) are the most common type of video. These are video versions of written blogs. They're short, regular, simple videos – like tips, for example – that you can share with your clients and your list. (Make sure you check out our free five-part video series to help you make a better video blog. You can find information about it at the end of this book.)

* * *

The benefit of being on camera yourself is that no one shares your passion, your drive, and your determination. You're the one whose eyes light up when you talk about your business, so if you were to put someone else on screen, they aren't likely to share your true passion and make it come across on camera as well as you do. I've talked to many people about whether they want to be on camera or find someone else to do it. I'll tell you what I tell them: I know that by you learning to be on camera yourself, you will have a massive transformation in confidence, in your communication, and in your business. When you can communicate your message in a powerful way, people listen. You'll find out how passionate you are about your business by going through this process.

The other benefit of being on camera is that you get to grow your confidence about how you look and start to embrace you the way you are. You also become aware of the clothing you wear! This self-awareness about how the rest of the world sees you can be useful. When you connect with people as your real self, you'll light up and you'll know you've touched someone's life with what you're doing and creating.

The upside of not being on camera is that you can hide behind everyone else. Whether you're in front of the camera or not, you can fully make that choice from a place of being confident. Most people who opt to be behind the scenes feel a need to do it, like me. Imagine if I had stayed small? I wouldn't be here now. I wouldn't have helped elephants, communities, or women around the world.

The key with all of the styles listed above is to know and imagine yourself in each situation. Try them on and see which one suits you. As video becomes more and more popular, these styles will start showing up more and more and video quality will also become better and better.

So, what's your Video Super Power and your video style? What drives you? Don't worry about the how for now, just focus on what excites you. The rest will take care of itself.

Girl Director Secret Technique

There's a secret way I teach my clients to be a director, and it's one of the best bangs for the buck. It will give you sooo many amazing things in one tip. You will:

- Get more subscribers
- Get more reviews
- Become a better director
- Gain camera confidence

If you want to know what it is, go to girldirector.com/GivingBack.

AUDIENCE CONNECTION

Visualize one person as you're speaking on camera. Talk as if you're having a conversation with them and you will touch their soul.

Now that you've done some work on what really drives you, it's time to refine your audience or, as we like to call it, your avatar, to make sure you have one and are, indeed, building one. You want people to watch your videos right?

You need to get inside your audience's mind so that you can make videos that really impact them. Because if you're talking to someone who's 30, you'll be communicating very differently and using different words and different ways of speaking and phrasing things than if you're talking to someone who's 60 or who's a teenager. That's why refining who you're speaking to is really important.

Finding out what will capture your audience's heart and imagination and incorporating that with your own passion will be *so* powerful. Even if you think you already know your audience, I suggest looking at this, because your audience evolves, just like you, and it's best to revisit this every six months or so.

Ninety percent of the people I speak to say they know their audience. Then they start working on it seriously and realize there's a major piece they'd been missing.

The biggest problem, I find, is when people say they can help everyone. Yes, that may be true, but if you want your business or your video to really sit well and impact the people you want it to, it's time to narrow down who you want to help. That doesn't mean you'll be ignoring people. You can always add different kinds of clients to the mix. Start with one focus and make that work first. Generally, I find that the person you want to help is someone like you. They have the same pain you had or the same problems you had and want help with moving to the next level. They usually have the same values as you, too.

Have you talked to the people around you, like your clients, to find out what kinds of videos would inspire them? There's no point in creating this amazing video if you're going find that no one in your market wants to learn that. Creating from the heart is one thing, but you must also have one ear to the ground and always be in touch with your clients. Ask them what they want to see from you. What would help them? What would inspire them? There's no need to reinvent the wheel – they have the content for you.

Imagine you're standing on a balcony. You see someone on the street and start yelling, "Hey, you!" and hope they will hear you and respond. However, if you speak directly to them as an individual, it's more likely that they'll answer. If you say, "Hey, you with the green shirt on!" it's more likely that the person in the green shirt will turn around. The same is true with your marketing: The more specifically you speak to the person watching the video, the more they'll relate to you.

The more you know how your audience ticks, where they

live, and what they like to do in their spare time, the better. And the deeper you look, the better. For example, our perfect avatar is a woman in her late 40s. She is a country girl at heart, but also loves to dress up. She has a certain edge about her that gives her a certain X factor. She is invisible on social media, but she's been working hard and wants to take on video. She's terrified of the camera, yet she knows she wants to do whatever is necessary to take things to the next level. She wants to create an online program to leverage herself and create stand-out videos that make her the rockstar of her industry. She's scared and doesn't know how it works, but has an inner knowing that this is the next step. She is quite spiritual and has done self-development, is an animal lover, and knows her calling is to make a bigger difference in the world with what she's been doing.

Having this as our avatar doesn't mean that we won't work with other people. It means that the clients we attract have some of these traits. Sometimes, they fit exactly.

I recommend sitting for a moment and writing out a paragraph about who this person is for you. Choose one to start with. Once you get that one right, you can expand from there.

* * *

To help you understand how it all works together, I want to share a story about what we did with our marketing that made a huge difference. We had Facebook ads that weren't getting results, and we weren't generating the leads we wanted. Even though I had done lots of work on our avatar, it wasn't really right for us until I asked one person who embodies our avatar, "What would make you click on this ad or landing page?" Bull's-eye. She explained what she'd want to be different, and we changed our ad. The next day, I couldn't believe how the click-through rate went through the roof on our Facebook ads and how many contact leads we started getting.

This adjustment, along with making videos that spoke directly to people wanting to know more about video, turned our business completely around. So, this is how powerful these tools are and how crucial this step is to get right. Really spend time thinking about it. The answers are all around you. You just need to listen to your clients more.

Max's Story

A well-known entrepreneur named Max came to work with us. She works with hundreds of women in her business. She does transformation work and runs a program with her own strategies.

When we started working with Max, she wanted to make videos but didn't even know where to start. She felt old and frustrated, because the videos she'd made were less than desirable. She wanted to be confident, to direct her own editing team, and to know what to set up at home so that her process worked each time. She had no connection to her audience and sales were suffering because of it. Basically, she had no idea what her audience really wanted.

Max told us she knew her audience, but when we went deeper and got more specific, she was blown away at the difference it made. This had been a *huge* missing piece for her in everything she was doing.

She had so many ideas and was overwhelmed and all over the place with her current marketing. She was spending thousands of dollars on production costs, but her brand and vision weren't aligned with or capturing her passion, so her messages weren't landing. She didn't get many views, and so the results of her videos weren't anything special. She had a YouTube channel, but didn't know what to do with it.

Once Max found out exactly what it was about her market that she was missing, she had so many light-bulb moments! Things really shifted for her in all ways.

Emotions

Once you start thinking about your audience (your avatar), things will start opening up. And once you've connected to who your audience is, it's time to put some emotion into what you're talking about. So many videos *tell* people what to do instead of *showing* them and attaching an emotion. If you want your video to have high impact, attach an emotion to it.

I bet you can remember the saddest movie you've ever watched or the most thought-provoking movie, or the video you saw that made you laugh the loudest.

Using your own stories is also important. This isn't just about teaching them stuff. It's about creating a connection with them. After all, they're buying *you*. The more vulnerable you are and the more you share, the more you'll attract people.

Some basic emotions are anger, fear, joy, excitement, happiness, silliness, surprise, and love. We get the best results when we post vulnerable, emotionally transparent posts on Girl Director's website, as well as from the sharing I do on social media. It's sometimes scary to share emotions, because we all want everyone to think we're doing well – but that isn't always what's real. Everyone has challenges, big and small, and it's through those challenges that we grow. We can see our own challenges as opportunities to help someone else.

Tapping into emotions was really hard for me, because for so long the medicine I was taking for narcolepsy dulled my emotions so I wouldn't collapse. My emotions still aren't at their full capacity, but they're getting better and better. When I share with people about what's going on with me, they love to hear it. Sharing emotions makes you relatable. It makes you real. Learning from your mistakes is what people are ultimately buying from you. Your videos are the same. Make sure you share from the heart about why your experience is important, about what worked, and about what didn't. For me, being honest and real on camera was really hard at first. But it was so worth it.

Lessons

To take your videos to the next level, the most important thing is to connect with your audience. It took me a while to get this, even though I've worked in the media industry for such a long time and knew logically what it meant to talk to a target market. But I didn't apply it myself. When I finally did, things shifted everywhere. It's profound when you get this. Things will really shift then for you too. Don't ignore this issue like I did for many years.

I've worked in advertising agencies and at big TV networks. They do this same work with their audience, no matter what the product is. The big production companies all know *exactly* who their targeted customer is. Open your fridge and every product you see has one type of person it is talking to. That doesn't mean you aren't going to talk to other people if they come to you, but it means you have a specific audience you're focusing on.

What it's all about is identifying the one problem you can help your ideal client solve. Having one intention. When you go in with an intention that's very focused, the *how* will take care of itself.

From now on, whenever you do a video, I want you to imagine that you're talking to your favourite client, the one client who inspires you the most, who gets the best results from what you give them, and who is implementing everything you're offering. How do you want them to feel at the end of your video?

When your mind chatter stops, you can focus on being present for what the person on the other side of the lens needs. Think of them and only them, and have a conversation with them on camera. Video is simply an extension of the same conversation you'd have in person. This technique will help you become more and more authentic and natural, just like you're really having a conversation. People will pay you if you're talking about what they're looking for and really want. As you talk and connect on your video, it's important to highlight the pain factor, so they can really see how they can benefit from what you're offering.

Okay, so how can you go that extra mile? Think about that as you create your video. Customer service. Honesty. Integrity. Personal messages when they least expect it. Think about how you like to be treated. How can you deliver great content and solutions to your particular avatar?

A Lesson in Mexico

Early in 2015, Michael and I traveled to the pyramids of Mexico. At the bottom of the pyramids, there were many stalls where people were selling things – everything from jewelry to clothing. You name it, it was there. But everyone sold the same thing in the same way. They'd all say, "Cheap! Cheap! Mine is cheaper."

I told Michael that if one of those stalls did something completely different and started to talk directly to their potential clients and ask them questions, it would make a huge difference. If they started targeting one person or one customer *type* and put up signs talking to them directly, they would have more success. If they made an effort to find out what the people passing by liked and what they loved and talked to them about their trip, they would be more likely to make sales, even if what they were selling was more expensive than the things being sold at the other stalls.

Marketing is crucial.

Creating the Perfect Video Script

Now I want to put all of this together and help you create a specific way of speaking to your avatar. Your client results are the key to writing your perfect video script. You need to be clear on the following:

1. What are the biggest problems/issues that your clients come to you for help with?
2. What are the biggest results and feelings they have after working with you?
3. What language and words do they use when they first come to you?

On a blank piece of paper, write down answers to the above questions, listing as many things as you can think of for each one. You want to get to know your clients intimately, to get inside their heads. The more you can empathize with them and feel their pain, their frustrations, and their desires, the better you'll be at marketing to them with your videos and showing them the way forward to working with you.

If you're just starting out in your business and don't have any results yet, for question two, above, speculate on what your client's results will be after working with you. Really drill down and think about what your clients want and what they would like to achieve by working with you.

Now that you have a good list of problems and results for questions 1 and 2, circle the three most common and biggest problems and the three most common and biggest results from your two lists.

Now you have what you need for the formula below. This will give you a simplified version of your video script.

Video Script Formula

1. Identify exactly who you're speaking to
2. Use their words and language *exactly*
3. Use conversational language, as if you're speaking to one person
4. Grab their attention by asking a question that relates directly to the biggest problems they have,
5. Describe what problems you solve and the results they will get for those problems after working with you
6. Have a strong call to action that will provide a way for them to start working with you

It takes some practice to get this right, so start simple. Begin with the problems they're having, and then tell how you can help solve those problems. The better you get at this type of script, the more creative you can be with your videos. Music and text is a powerful way to go when it comes to telling a story.

We use our script as the basis for our Facebook ads and landing pages. In fact, we use it for most of our marketing, in one way or another, as it really draws people in and taps into their core needs. The script doesn't solve their issues then and there – that would be unrealistic. Instead, it's a call to action that leads them to us so that we can start helping them to solve their issues.

Give it a go with your marketing and let us know what happens. From this basic concept of your Perfect Script, you can then make your videos more complex by developing the conversation, the emotion, the music, and whatever else you're drawn to include in your video. This is a great start.

Girl Director Secret Technique

If you want to download more amazing scripts we've used and take this concept to the next level, go to girldirector.com/PerfectScript.

USING VIDEO FOR MARKETING

Compare your videos only to the ones you've made before.

The Future of Marketing

I'll let you in on a prediction I have about where marketing in general is heading. In the not-too-distant future, I believe businesses will be focusing on creating documentaries or short, community-focused videos that are aligned with company or individual values and beliefs.

People are bombarded with soulless marketing that isn't deep or engaging. We'll start moving toward deeper messages, messages with purpose that educate. People are traveling more and are exposed to more stories in the world. Technology is becoming easier and more accessible to use.

Video is only going to get bigger and bigger, so the sooner you embrace what video can do, the better you will be in the long run. I know how you feel right now. I get how overwhelming it is when you're just starting. But if you start making videos today, then every single video you make will be better than the last.

It's more than likely that your videos won't look like Emmy Award-winners when you start. It takes time to master a new skill. Making videos is a skill that will come in very handy in so many ways. So stick with it. Watch and learn.

A little rule I have for myself is that with every single video I make, I set the intention to learn something new and try something different in order to lift the quality, whether that's by working in a new location, using a cool gadget, shooting from a new angle, adding text, or using great music.

Every single person sees the world in their own unique way, so embrace that and carry what's unique about you into your videos. If you keep thinking your videos are never good enough, they won't be. Try thinking the opposite instead.

With so many more people marketing their businesses and offering free stuff and video blogs, there will be a tipping point. In order to stand out from everyone else, I recommend getting ahead of the game by starting to make videos as soon as you can.

Tap into Your Local Resources

Go out into your local community and find a story. You're surrounded by inspiring people doing inspiring things. You can make a video about them with your phone.

Find something that you're drawn to in your local community. Find somewhere local where you could make a video. There are stories everywhere you turn. Ask around and you'll find lots of great things to create a video about. Find something that's aligned with you, your brand, and/or your beliefs, and include that in your video.

Here are some benefits of making a video in your community:

- Free marketing
- Improved video skills
- Being seen as the expert
- Helping a cause that has meaning and emotion behind it

We did this ourselves recently with a community project aligned with our values. We made a little music video with the community and involved the local council, a young children's choir, local Girl Guides, and local artists – all to build awareness to help save local birds. Making that video served these purposes:

- We helped a cause that's important to us
- We taught young girls how to use video for marketing
- We met people outside our circle
- We were seen as the experts
- We got free PR on radio and in the newspaper
- We brought new people to our website and they were interested in what we were doing

Can you see now why this kind of thing works so well?

Right now, I'd like you to think about what part of your community you could call on to help you do a video. Maybe it's a retirement home or a school. Go there and speak to someone and ask them to tell their story.

There are infinite opportunities around you. Even if you only film one interview and take a few different shots outside the place where you did the interview, in order to help you tell the story, that's all you need.

Tara's Story

Sharing stories is often the best way to see opportunities for yourself. Seeing what happened for others is one of the biggest ways I learn, and it has help me with all of the personal development I've done. I want to share a story from one of our clients.

Tara has a great business. She and her husband own a camel-trekking company in Australia. She wanted to learn video, but didn't know where to start. Her goal was to have more people come on treks and to make more money. After eight weeks of working with the ideas and techniques we taught her, Tara had made videos for her business that created so much Facebook engagement that her treks were booked well in advance. Later, she created a video Cameleer training course and charged $3000 per person. She also made a video to help end child sex slavery, raising $15k from the video and her own PR. Not a bad effort!

Tara has also been able to show the outback on her videos, so her viewers more clearly see how amazing the landscape is. She engaged with people so they could see and feel that experience for themselves. Other companies have been trying to copy her, but by now she and her husband are at the top of their game with their company.

Tara's Tools. Tara started by using her iPhone and a simple lapel microphone that you can buy on eBay. As long as you have a tripod and good lighting and sound, you're sorted. The rest is up to you and what your clients are looking for in a video style. From her iPhone, Tara moved on to a higher-quality camera – a Canon DSLR (a digital single-lens reflex camera) – once she understood the basic principles of making videos. This isn't about how expensive your camera is. You can make amazing videos on your phone if you have all the elements I've mentioned already. It really is all about understanding the concepts of video. Then the audience connection, the emotion, the style, and all the rest will come together and flow.

Alba's Story

Alba is an image consultant with an engineering background. She wanted an online program she could sell, and she wanted to make videos that communicated to her clients who she is and what she's doing. It was important for her to present well and for her videos to match her image and brand. As you can imagine, since Alba is an image consultant, it was important for her to look the part. She created the videos herself using her phone and simple software on her computer.

To help her videos stand out even more, I gave her some ideas about editing, suggesting that she add some still images and some fast shots of herself, along with camera sound effects. That added to the customer's experience.

Alba's image and style on screen are a huge draw, as colours and clothing make a big impact on the way you look on camera. Think about those moments when someone told you how amazing you looked in a particular colour. Perhaps it's time to pull out those colours and experiment with them.

The first week Alba's video advert went up, she got 100 leads on Facebook. She said everyone kept saying they could see her everywhere online.

The great thing is that Alba now feels confident about making videos, so now she can either create the videos herself or ask someone else to shoot them. She knows the language and how things should look. Her videos look better and better every time I see them.

Alba's Tools. She used an iPhone, her computer, LED Lighting, and a lapel microphone. She already had a strong brand and that gave her videos that extra edge.

Two Types of Video Marketing

There are two types of video marketing I recommend focusing on: the type that brings you more leads and the type that keeps people engaged. It doesn't matter if you're a rockstar, promoting a feature film, or building a business or a product – marketing is important. How you represent yourself is important. Bringing in leads and keeping your customers engaged is about building a relationship and building trust.

You should always be marketing – educating people, giving value, or entertaining, and building up a following of like-minded people.

Video Campaigns

Video campaigns are appearing in most forms of social media now, as well as on websites and even on our mobile phones. Video is becoming bigger and bigger.

When you create a video campaign, you want to make sure it's full of valuable content. If the content is only okay, then, in my experience, it's not going to work. If you're really tapped into what your clients need, then the content of your videos should be easy for you to come up with.

Video campaigns need a firm strategy. We've found that it's important to know how to create a strategy for yourself before you give your video campaign over to someone else to manage for you. A couple of our clients outsourced the strategy process and found that when they weren't getting results, they didn't know what to do to change things. So they stopped the campaign, when all it really needed was some fine tuning to get it back on track. Now they're doing the strategizing themselves and they outsource the process, knowing what needs to be changed and tweaked if that's needed.

We've grown our whole business from two successful video campaigns on Facebook. If you get the process right and follow our system, you can quickly grow your database.

Video connects you to people so much faster than anything else. Yes, it takes a little while to set up completely, but the rewards are greater, especially when your videos keep running and working for you.

I always recommend that clients think of a great, inspirational idea to share in a video. Do it. Do it fast! Get your videos out there.

Types of video campaigns out there right now:

- Building leads
- Keeping engagement
- Product launches
- Book trailers
- Entertainment
- Awareness

There are lots of ways you can connect to people with video when you're creating a video campaign strategy. I've listed some of them below.

Building Leads with Videos

Here are a few cool ideas to get you inspired about the kinds of videos you can make to grow your community and get leads:

- Run a video series on social media
- Send personal video messages to clients
- Run competitions

- Turn a webinar into a series and market that
- Make a trailer for your product or book
- Create a crowd funding campaign
- Create an interview series for subscribers

There are so many cool things you can do.

Building Engagement with Videos

Building engagement with video is when you use your videos to keep your audience inspired about what you're doing once you get clients in your database. You give them great information, sharing with them about yourself and your business so that they can connect more readily to what you're doing. Engagement videos can be video series, video blogs, video blooper collections, launches, video interviews, and lots more. The thing most people get wrong is they don't constantly engage with the people in their database. We see massive results once a client commits to sending out regular, entertaining videos.

Video Series

A video series is a series of videos in the same style or theme. For the best outcome, release them weekly at the same time to build consistency. Think of a TV series, for example. Your viewer can have some consistency and build it into their week.

Marie Forleo's Q & A videos are a series. A video blog is also a type of series. Our Million Dollar Women is a brilliant series of interviews with million-dollar business women. Have a look at our YouTube page to see the different videos there: youtube.com/girldirectorTV.

You can make a video series where you interview other

people and offer lots of cool stuff your clients will love. All you need is twenty seconds of courage to call the first person and book a time for the interview. Then do it! I love living from this idea of twenty seconds of courage that I mentioned earlier. I use this trick all the time. Imagine if you had twenty seconds of courage to call someone you wanted to connect with or do something (like schedule an interview for a video) without letting the fear stop you. How different would your results be? You never know if you don't give it a go. Grab your pen now and write a list of the people you would like to interview. I did this very thing for our elephant documentary. I had interviews in London, Thailand and Africa – some with people who never usually do interviews. Go for it. You can do it. Let me know what happens.

Video Blogs

Video blogs are the simplest engagement videos you can do. They're great for sending out to a new person in your community or client. Video blogs are either life blogging or they are "how to videos". Consistency is the key. Keep people engaged by talking about things in short 2-5 minute videos. Keep them wanting more each week. It doesn't matter what platform you choose to use. Choose one to start with and build your audience from there. If you can add story elements to your videos this will help drive engagement even more. Create suspense, surprise or keep them guessing. This formula always works for creating more engagement.

Video Messages

You can email videos to your list to ask them questions and find out what they may be struggling with, or to send them short messages. I like to surprise people and keep things personal and different. Perhaps you can set up a welcome sequence for when someone joins your database – a little video to welcome them so they feel more connected to you.

YouTube

YouTube is the perfect place to create your video marketing machine. Even with 300+ hours of videos uploaded every minute on YouTube there is still room for you to grow. Most channels aren't optimized properly and there are gaps. Big secret here is, *What ONE subject do you want to be known for?* If you want our strategy with growing your channel you can talk to us. We have clients with small channels and others with over 500k subs. They are all using the Channel to profoundly grow their visibility and business. You don't need millions of subscribers to have a successful following or business.

Facebook

If you have a business with a Facebook presence (and I'm assuming you do), you may have noticed how much more exposure you can gain for your business by having video on your Facebook page. With Facebook, posting regular videos is key. We post on both YouTube and Facebook, depending on the strategy. Secrets to creating powerful videos on most platforms are; Start with a compelling title or reason for someone to watch, tell them what the video is going to be about, get into the content and (IMPORTANT) make sure you have a call to action.

TikTok

This is a great platform to have fun and go viral fast. Here are some key areas to remember with this platform... Be consistent in your message and post regularly each day. Use the challenges once per week as a way of going viral. Use popular music as another way to be noticed. Remember to take your audience over to your other platforms or database so you are in control of the outcome you want.

Live Video Streaming

Live video streaming is what it sounds like: you're recording live and people can interact with you in real time. Applications such as Streamyard mean you can now make a TV show and stream in multiple places. We streamed a 2-hour entertainment show while we were in lock down. It was a fantastic way to showcase clients, add a musical element and help you to be seen. If you don't like LIVE, don't do it. People can sense it if you aren't confident or don't like something. There are many ways to deliver great content.

* * *

Marketing is the single most important thing you can do for your business – even when you're busy and things are going well. Without letting people know who you are and what you're about, how are they going to find you?

I spoke to someone recently who'd built a beautiful business and thought that when she opened the doors, customers would just come in. No! You want to market ahead of time. Create a buzz. It takes a few weeks for momentum to build. When you have that momentum, keep it up from there.

The dollars you spend on marketing must give you a clear return on your investment. That means tracking what you do and checking out the data. For us, Facebook has been by far the most successful platform. We make ten times what we spend on Facebook ads.

Now it's your turn to choose a platform and go for it. You can do it! Remember that with every video you make, you'll get better and better. I promise.

Here are the must-have videos for your business. When you start doing videos, start with these:

- Video testimonials
- Video campaigns
- Regular engagement video each week

Put these together first, then create more and more videos to slowly replace the text you've been using online. Just do it.

Your videos don't have to be perfect. I tell you, every single person in the TV and film industry all say the same thing: that their first videos looked awful. *Everyone's* videos look terrible and embarrassing when they start out. The important thing is to just start. You'll learn from every single video you make. You'll tweak and adjust what you do and the technology you use. Being afraid of making mistakes will only hinder your process. I love mistakes, because that's how I improve things for the next time!

Girl Director Secret Technique

The best place to start is by doing a video blog. Make it short, simple, and with content that's of value. Make them regularly and you'll see a massive shift in your results. Check out our special, detailed video blog training: girldirector.com/BetterVideoBlogs.

CREATE CLIENTS

Your mind is the most powerful moviemaker of all.

In this chapter, I'm going to talk about the best ways to boost your income with video and how to find more clients. After all, you want to make money by being a change-maker so you can do the things you want to do, right? Let's face it, if you're going to spend the time, money, and energy on learning video, you want to get a return on that investment.

There are multiple ways of making money with video. Your choices depend on your overall strategy.

My suggestion is to focus on helping the people who inspire you the most. Those are the people you've had the biggest results with in the past.

As I said before, your ideal client is like you, but a few years earlier. You're here to save people from making the same mistakes you did. You're here to guide them.

It's important to feel proud of everything you put out there. Confidence in your videos attracts people. Not feeling confident doesn't. Always turn up your energy and get into the right mindset before turning on the camera. You can do this by playing music or doing whatever gets you feeling excited about the people you want to reach. Something I do just before I press record is visualize how perfect the video will be. It sets up a good outcome to visualize the results first. Try it!

I'll share with you now a couple more stories about clients who have profoundly grown from implementing video projects, just as we at Girl Director have. Everything we teach our clients is exactly what we do ourselves.

Kerri's Story

When I met Kerri, I saw a very confident women who knew her stuff. She was like a rock chick in the shamanic healer world. She got profound results working with her one-on-one clients, but she wanted to reach more people. Her work is done privately, so she was finding it really hard to figure out how to communicate what she did in her marketing, and also because she works with ancient techniques and it felt hard to explain.

When Kerri came to us, she found technology difficult. She didn't want to get it wrong and had fears of messing it up. As we started working more closely with Kerri, what became more and more apparent was that she felt really uncomfortable on camera and didn't like it when she saw her videos. Her image never matched the person she expected to see looking back at her. It broke my heart to see how beautiful she was on camera and know that she couldn't see it yet. She wasn't used to seeing her image and she also felt overwhelmed by the technology.

Kerri didn't want to put herself out there unless her image and brand reflected her business. But her brand was also out of alignment. She knew how important video was for her in order to be seen as the expert in her field, but she didn't think it possible to be paid well for what she did without having to do it one-on-one.

Boy, did she get a surprise! Because Kerri already had proven results with her clients, we were able to harness what she was doing to create an online program for which clients now pay thousands of dollars to work with her. Pretty cool, huh? She's now so excited about what's possible for her life. She can work less and actually reach and help more clients.

It all started with Kerri having the confidence at one of our live events to work with us for a few hours. She worked through her fears one by one. and they disappeared. (There's a special treat at the end of this chapter to help you if you're struggling with being seen.) Kerri started owning the camera and attracting more clients. It was the most profound change I've ever seen. Her Facebook posts alone had so much engagement. So did her ads. Her first webinar was packed with people, and that's something that rarely happens the first time out.

Friends were stopping Kerri in the street, wanting to know what she was doing in her life because she looked so good. Whatever it was, they said, she should keep doing it, because it was amazing. Her confidence was growing and her clients were getting even more incredible results.

This is what stepping into your power looks like. This is what happens when you make a shift and free yourself from the invisible forces that have been holding you back. You attract more clients who you're meant to help because you're connecting to them with your authentic voice.

Can you remember a time when you felt amazing? When you felt untouchable and on top of your game? A time when you were bursting with confidence? Exactly how did you feel in that moment? How were you standing and holding yourself? I want you to remember that moment anytime you're scared of the camera. Step back into that place where you owned it!

Kerri's Tools. She used an iPhone, LED lights, a lapel microphone, camera confidence tools, iMovie on the Mac, and a DSLR camera.

Strategy, Vision, and Intention

Producing great video content and creating digital assets you can sell is one of the best things you can do to leverage yourself. Because once those videos are done, you can create marketing to sell them, whether that's through online programs, by emailing links to the videos, or selling webinars. It all depends on your strategy.

If you aren't sure what strategy you want to use, don't wait and tie yourself in knots thinking about it. Email me at iwantvideos@girldirector.com instead, and let's chat. Don't do what I did and hire a business planner who wasn't right for me, who talked me into changing my Girl Director name, and who didn't understand my business. That cost me money and time that I'll never get back. I wish I'd had the support that's available now back when I was struggling.

If you're part of a multi-level marketing business, video can help you massively, too. I haven't seen many people fully embrace using it well, so if you do, you can capture a large percentage of the market, because you're connecting well with your clients. It will take some time and planning, but it all comes down to the strategy.

Something we love about video is that we can create high-quality digital assets to sell. We used to do this through CDs and DVDs. Now, with video, people can download our information, which is better because we can track who's using it and where it's going. We can also change and update our content without having to update all the DVDs.

Packaging up your magic into a video is the key. Then you can sell things online and work from anywhere!

Membership Sites

Creating a successful membership site is all about creating a great customer user experience. Think about Apple or Virgin. You want the experience to be amazing and take customers on a journey from the moment they sign up with you.

Packaging and leveraging are keys to making more money with video. Video allows you to step away from only doing one-on-one. You can also charge more if you have great video content on your site, because you've added more value. The higher-end your videos are, and the more value they give, the better your offering and so the more you can charge for what you do.

You can either create a low-end offer and start small or start with higher end offers and work with fewer people. If you're an expert at what you do, it makes sense to work with fewer people and focus on helping them to get the results they desire by using great videos.

Facebook Communities

I love Facebook communities. On Facebook, Girl Director has a thriving community of women making videos. Come over to our Facebook page to connect with the latest news. It's at https://www.facebook.com/GirlDirector/. If you have any questions or things you want to share, come on over.

What I love about our Facebook participants is that I get to see what they're all creating and I can mentor them in the group. When they post their videos, I can see straight away what isn't working and what is. Sharing their videos gives them more experience with posting and getting used to the technology.

We also post little video challenges on Facebook from time to time, to keep people engaged and to keep their creative minds ever-expanding, so they keep looking for ways to stand out and add extra value to their businesses. The quality of videos coming out of this community is amazing!

Live Webinars and Masterclasses

Webinars are a great way to do classes online, especially if you don't have enough time to film a video series. You can run a webinar and a Facebook community to deliver your content with slides and interact. You can also record the webinar content and release it as a program at a later date. Videos that engage your list is still the most effective way to build trust and connection.

Documentary

If you're drawn to create a documentary, know that this is a longer-term investment. Doing a documentary will bring you exposure and boost your income through the PR and increased marketing power. The challenges you overcome and the other things you can offer from having learned during your own experience will also add to your bottom line.

Before you even start your documentary, it's important to know who you're going to be talking to as an audience and build a following. The more you can implement the other things I talk about in this book, the better the results will be for your documentary.

BETTER VIDEOS

* * *

Making more money with video requires constant connection and engagement with your clients. You must have some way of collecting people's details and email addresses. Knowing your metrics on your social media sites – such as your Facebook likes and views – can help with getting you sponsorship deals (even though you don't own Facebook likes as a list to which you have direct access).

You want to grow your list of ideal clients as fast as possible. They are who you want to send your videos to each week, so you can connect and engage with them via great content. The more subscribers you get on social media, the more you can approach companies for sponsorship deals and other mutually beneficial things.

* * *

As I mentioned above, creating digital assets is the key. Whether you create a video series to sell or videos to use for your marketing, the videos you create won't go to waste. If a video doesn't work in one place, use it somewhere else, like on your website as a giveaway, or as a lead magnet.

The best thing to do is to find something the market wants, sell it and *then* create it. There's no point in creating it unless you've sold it, because then you know for sure it's wanted.

Keep asking yourself, "What do my customers want?" Think about your clients' experience as they watch your videos. How do you want them to feel? What is your intention?

Girl Director Secret Technique

Do you like to ask for money? It won't matter how good your videos are if you don't feel great about asking for payment. This is a huge issue I had to overcome.

Do you want to download an exercise to help you shift this? If so, go to: girldirector.com/PaperEnergy.

SABOTAGING SUCCESS

The clearer the movie in your mind, the more likely it will happen.

I am so proud of you for getting this far. Well done. Let's go over what you've learned so far. You're clear on your Video Super Power. You now get how *important* video is to use in your business right *now*. You also have some insight into where the market is going. You know what to do to make money using video. You have more confidence on camera.

You've come this far, but it wouldn't be fair of me to say that everything is going to be easy from this point. Sometimes people get really excited and pumped after talking to me or coming to one of our workshops and what happens next is that they do nothing.

Others will get as far as making one video. Then they'll see themselves in the video and freak out. And then there are people who won't do anything but read and read more information.

Please don't be one of those people who don't implement.

Don't let your fears talk you out of what you really want for yourself. It really saddens me how many people don't have the lives they really want, when all it comes down to is taking action.

The best thing I've done in my life has been to work with mentors. A good mentor teaches you, pushes you, guides you, and sees you bigger than you see yourself. It can be so much easier to know what to do when you have someone in front of you on the path, teaching you how to not make the same mistakes they did.

As you read in my story, my journey hasn't been easy for me. I lost my job, I've had to deal with an illness that made me sleep all the time, I had a nervous breakdown. But I came back by using all the tools in this book and by using three things that have helped me succeed: determination, passion, and wanting to make a difference. Without those, I wouldn't have gotten here – and I'm very glad I'm here.

Fears are normal. Hey, I have fears all the time, but I don't let them rule me. The people you want to help need your support. You can do every single thing you want to do and more, but you need to move ahead through your fears.

Not only do people make one video and then give up, they do a video Facebook advert, spend $20 to put it up, and stop when it doesn't work. They say, "Oh, it's too hard," because there are underlying fears they're not dealing with. It isn't too hard if you're truly dedicated to helping the people you want to help. Video is *the thing* that is the fastest way to connect with people. Why not learn to do it and do it well? Those half-attempts that you aren't proud of aren't going to help you stand out and be a rockstar. But they're a good start!

A girl came to one of our workshops, and afterwards I kept track of her process and watched her stuff, as I do from time to time (I like to see how you're doing). I messaged her a couple of times because I could see that she was struggling.

She was all over the place with her message. She ended up stopping and doing nothing. A year later, she came back in a worse position because she had more fears and concerns about moving forward. We worked together and, in a short space of time, she was on track, making videos that were attracting the right clients and getting leads. Can you see how much time she would have saved by reaching out sooner? Don't let this be you. Okay, promise me you'll stick with this. You'll be so grateful you did.

I want to share an incredible story of what courage looks like, despite so many things happening that get in the way.

Helen's Story

Helen came to us with great ideas about where she wanted to take her business. She's a make-up artist in her mid-50s – an amazing woman and a diva. She wanted to use video to communicate powerfully and entertainingly about the fun side of make-up and styling, but her message and her marketing weren't there. She was frustrated because she wanted to create a business for her retirement and stop teaching at high school, but hadn't been able to do that.

Helen didn't have a consistent message aligned with where she wanted to go and her brand wasn't highlighting who she really was. At the beginning, she really struggled with technology and found it really difficult to remember things because of a brain injury she'd had. At times, Helen would go really quiet and I'd think she'd given up, but she was just thinking and trying to remember.

Throughout the process of learning to make great videos, Helen struggled at times and wanted to give up. Her courage and determination were amazing. She learned video editing and how to create her website. She said that before she worked with us, she used to ask her sons to help, but they would just shrug their shoulders. Now, after taking matters in her own hands, she's confident with technology. She's switched from a PC to a Mac computer, and all her videos have class and style and are well-branded. The transformation that happened to Helen as she went through our process was incredible. She completely changed her business model and took on all the learning she needed to do. She worked through the process, came out the other side, and is now directing her own video shoots. She runs workshops helping women with their style onscreen and also teaches them in front of the camera.

By sticking with her vision, Helen has created a business, and video has given that business an edge that other make-up artists and stylists don't have. She's a rockstar at what she does. She stands out. Her marketing is so different and entertaining that she's getting more and more business. People love her. She owns the camera.

Helen's story shows that no matter what age you are, you can have style and attitude and completely own what you do. It also shows that no matter what age you are or what has happened in your life, you can keep going. It may take longer than you expected, but you must keep going with your goals. With the right support, you can do anything.

Girl Director Secret Technique

Would you like to watch a video of me talking through my own special way of doing vision boards? No one else does them quite the same. I've seen amazing results with what happens when people use vision boards in this way. To get this video lesson go to girldirector.com/SecretVideo-Technique.

BE THE ROCKSTAR OF YOUR MESSAGE

You don't need to be a musician to be rockstar.

For this chapter, I want you to bring out your inner rockstar. Think about what kind of rockstar you're going to step into as you read. When I say the word "rockstar," I'm talking about the *personality* of any kind of musician in any genre. Rockstars come in all shapes and sizes and play all kinds of music. There are the obvious rockstars, like Jim Morrison, Madonna, David Bowie, Lady Gaga, and Michael Hutchence, but don't forget about the less obvious ones, like Luciano Pavarotti, Grace Jones, Miles Davis, and André Rieu. Even Yoko Ono and Nana Mouskouri are unique rockstars in their own ways.

What attitude do you want to adopt by being a rockstar? What kind of style would you have as a rockstar? What cause are you going to support? It's time to stand up and feel the inner rockstar that sets you apart from the others in your industry.

So, how does it feel to be a rockstar? What power do you need to tap into in order for your inner rockstar to show up on camera, in your business, and to your audience?

What do Russell Brand, Tony Robbins, Steve Jobs, Richard Branson, and Marco Pierre White all have in common? They are all rockstars in their industry.

Of course, you want to have an edge over other businesses. Now that you're armed with all kinds of production tricks, scripts, and ways to make more money with video, let's ramp it up to another notch.

If you want to be a rockstar in what you're doing, you have to be an expert, no question about it. There's no point in trying to be a rockstar if you only dabble in a few things here and there. If you want to stand out, then pick the one thing you are the *best* at and stick with it.

One thing I've been guilty of (and that I still do, at times) is taking on too many projects beyond what I'm best at. Some of us can have a habit of over-complicating things.

Remember that simple is best. When you're an expert and you know it, you have confidence about what you do. If you aren't already *the* expert at what you do, what can you do to make sure that you are? What other skills can you get? What can you tap into so that you can be the expert? What specific niche can you fill in your market? The more you can niche yourself, the better.

Rockstars have confidence. They have their own unique style. They have videos, they have a devoted audience, and they have marketing. They do events and tours. As an entrepreneur, you are exactly the same.

* * *

Rockstars also have music. In this chapter, we're going to explore music and how powerful it is. Music is the missing ingredient in most of the videos I watch. I instantly switch off when I hear the same type of music over and over again. You want music for your video that's thought-provoking, emotional, and pattern-interrupting.

Music helps your message. Many videos I see online today use music as an afterthought. Music helps you build emotion. Have ever tried watching a horror movie with the sound turned down? There's a massive difference, isn't there?

You can also use different sound effects to enhance your videos. For one burger advert I worked on, instead of using music I added the sound effects of a construction site. As the burger was being built, there were sound effects of trucks, cranes, and workmen yelling. That's an example of what you can do with sound to change the dynamics of a production.

Having created so many music videos (and through my work with Symphony of the Earth), I've watched and studied many musicians over the years. It also helps that Michael's a musician. There are so many similarities between musicians and successful business people, because they often have the same drive, passion, and ambition.

I love stepping into my own inner rockstar. I love wearing the leather pants and cool tops (Though I must say that leather pants are a bit harder to pull off in the hotter climate we live in these days!).

Your environment is also a big factor when it comes to making videos and inspiring you to step into being a rockstar in your industry. Michael and I live in an incredible house that feels like a rockstar's mansion. It's perfect for clients to stay in, and it has loads of natural light coming in all day. There are many great spaces to film here, and we're surrounded by bush, with views reaching right down to the sea. It's pretty cool. We like having a space to live in that inspires us to be rockstars.

In the past, when I lived in a smaller space, my mindset

shrank down to meet the size and style of the house. When we first moved into our current house, we didn't know how we were going to make it work because it was so much different and bigger, but we did it. We're grown into this bigger, better space, both mentality and as a lifestyle.

The ROCKSTAR Process

When we work with our clients, we take them through our special ROCKSTAR process, which looks like this:

- **R**ealize your magic and know what you believe
- **O**rganize your ideas
- **C**reate the look you want
- **K**it up with the gear you need
- **S**hoot your footage
- **T**ransform your footage into quality, ROCKSTAR videos
- **A**ctivate your marketing funnel
- **R**eap the rewards

Realize your magic. This is where you harness your expertise and make sure you're *focusing on one thing powerfully*. This can be hard to do if you're an idea person, like me. The trick is to simplify, so you get right down to what you do best.

Organize your ideas. Plan out everything to do with your videos and your message, including the music. We can help with this.

Create the look you want. This is about creating your video brand, your style, and everything to do with the look and style of your videos, including the locations and how you dress. Your videos carry an energy. There is much in the unseen energy of video as there is in the visual side.

If you haven't been to a stylist or had your colours done, I recommend doing so. It's a great investment and doesn't have to be expensive. Go to a fashion design school or a college design department and ask for help. They're usually very open to helping people. I did this when Girl Director started in 2005.

If you watch a reality music show or talent show, check out the clothing. That's a major part of who the performers are. What stand-out style feature can you introduce to your videos and your marketing? Do you have a unique style or design? Perhaps you can buy some unusual jewelry. That's one of the big things I did when I updated my style recently. There's quite a science to branding your style!

Kit up with the gear you need. There's a core set of equipment needed for every shoot (I'll talk more about this later), but every video is slightly different and sometimes you may need a few new tricks or toys to enhance the video you're creating.

Shoot your footage. The planning and pre-production stages all come together here at the shoot. Shooting is the fun part, and *fun* is an important aspect of the ROCKSTAR video process!

Transform your footage into quality, ROCKSTAR videos. Once the shooting is done, the editing process begins, and all of the jigsaw pieces get put together to make your video look and sound great.

Activate your marketing funnel. Videos won't do you any good without a marketing plan. After all, if you compare a music video to a business video, a music video is just a marketing video for a band. We apply a similar strategy here.

Reap the rewards. Watch what happens when you put

videos out there that you're proud of. Watch the leads come in. Start connecting with your new clients.

* * *

As you can see, this is an easy approach. It's the process we follow when working with clients. All you have to do is keep calm and trust the process.

Be sure to use music tracks that you've purchased (which you can do online) or to use royalty-free music from Creative Commons. If you're editing on YouTube, you can get a list of music options there that you can use. Some bands let you use their tracks in exchange for crediting the band at the end of the video. Using a popular music track can cost a fortune. If you wanted to use music by Gwen Stefani or Robbie Williams, it could cost $10k to $40k for a license. Facebook will remove the video from your feed if you use copyrighted music. You can even be banned or be shut down if you breach their terms.

Girl Director Secret Technique

Find three music tracks you feel like you could step into. They must inspire you and evoke a feeling and a vision for your video. Three tracks is a great number to begin with. Use one of these tracks on every video you make, to create a familiar sound for your videos. This will help you create your own soundtrack that people will recognize as part of your brand.

If you want the latest links to the best music tracks on the planet so you can explore to find your own personal soundtrack, go to girldirector.com/YourSoundtrack.

MAKING STAND-OUT VIDEOS

It's not how expensive your camera is, but how you use it that counts.

Now you're ready to give a few things a try with our little master class in production. The video-making techniques in this chapter have been the same for as long as I can remember (and most of them also apply when shooting still photographs). I suggest you go out and play. Take some still photographs first, and then transfer what you already know to creating videos. Be curious. Have a playful attitude. Video and photography is all about finding your own creative style and edge. All of the tips and tricks here will definitely help your videos stand out from the masses.

Gear

We've done the hard work for you and created a perfect list of stuff we use, along with the relevant links, saving you hours. You can grab your own copy here: girldirector.com/GearlLst.

The *must*-have things in your video tool kit are:

1. Tripod (we love the Manfrotto brand)
2. Lapel (also called lavalier) microphone (and an adapter for your smartphone)
3. Camera – iPhone/smartphone or DSLR
4. Lighting – softboxes or LED lights, depending on the space you have and the look you want; both are great, for different reasons.

Lighting is a fine art. Don't worry if you muck it up at first. Lighting crews take a long time to set up on every professional shoot I've ever been involved in. Even the outside shoots. On the set of every music video I directed, the lighting guys would take two to three hours every time we changed the set.

You don't have to buy all the gear at once. Start with the tripod and microphone, and then get the lights. Your videos will look amazing when you use even just this simple, must-have, non-expensive gear. Dressing well and having great make-up and lighting will all help you look like a million dollars (you can go to a make-up counter at a store to get your make-up done!).

Locations

A good location can make a huge difference. Sometimes all you need to do is to find an awesome location, film it well, and then BAM! Your video level just went up two notches. I used to spend a lot of time looking for great locations.

Times of day can affect your location, so make sure you

check out beforehand where the sun will be coming from at the time of day you want to shoot.

Look around your neighborhood for great spots. Remember that things look different from behind the lens. I like to grab my iPhone and go wandering around taking photos so I can see what things look like from the lens.

Locations inside a studio or a house can be interesting, too. You can create a background to use for your video blogs. There are plenty of cool garages out there that have interesting textures on the outside that you can use as backgrounds to shoot against.

Good props are another great way of enhancing the location and making it more interesting.

Backgrounds

You've probably seen webcam videos shot against a blank wall for a background. You can easily do that, but how about shooting against something else? Backgrounds are everywhere you look. I suggest going around your house and office and finding three different scenes you love. Make sure they're simple. The background could be a specific colour, a scene, a wooden texture, or a background you've created yourself.

Perhaps you want to shoot on a green screen and add your own stock image. If you're in a small apartment with no great background, this is a great way to add more depth to what you're doing. Using a green screen is a great way to create an illusion.

Your background gives a clear impression of where you are. The space you're in is part of creating an image for yourself. You can use things like TV monitors, images in frames, statues, or nature in your background. Just remember to minimise distracting things in the background.

Keep one important rule in mind when it comes to backgrounds: Simple is best. Never have a crowded scene as a background. You want people to see and pay attention to *you* instead of being distracted by the background.

Shooting Outdoors

Golden hour is my favourite time of day to film. It's also the best time to film silhouettes. The lighting is soft and golden during this time of day – thus the name. Golden hour is the time just after dawn or just before dusk. Depending on where you are on the planet and the time of year, golden hour is somewhere between 5 a.m. and 7 a.m., and then between 4 p.m. and 6 p.m. You have a small window to film at this time of day, so you want to be ready before golden hour starts and then move fast!

Know Your Platform

There are so many more platforms you can use today. Vertical videos, stories, blogs, podcasts, IGTV, YouTube. How on earth do you keep up? Often people get overwhelmed thinking they need to be on every single one. Pick 2 and stick to them. The other thing you can do is do what we call "batch content". This is when you have one filming day and film enough videos for the month. It is building a process into the business so you can record all your videos and edit them for different formats. There are great apps now that allow you to upload your videos and export them for each different platform.

Mixed Camera Shots

When you watch videos you'll see the three main shot types listed below used most frequently. There are others but stick with these and get them right before getting moving on. To make your videos flow better, have these shots types in your edited version (depending on how simple you want your videos to be):

- **Wide Shot (WS).** The whole scene, from your head to your toes. This is how you set the scene by filming landscapes or parts of the location environment.
- **Medium Close-Up (MCU).** This is a shot of the head and shoulders – like a newsreader on TV. This is the standard "talking head" position you see in most video blogs. The difference with yours, from now on, is that you'll also be adding the other types of shots to make your videos more interesting.
- **Close-Up (CU).** Don't be afraid to come up really close to the camera. I like to film half of my face on camera. It helps you to connect with people when you're talking about something important. In the music videos I've directed, there are lots of shots where the camera goes up really close to someone's face.

The Rule of Nine

If you don't already know this rule, learning it will change your life forever. After I found out about this rule, I realized that I'd already been taking photos using the rule of nine. Sometimes using it is instinctive, and it may be for you, too.

Here's how it works: The next time you're taking a photo, imagine that there's an imaginary grid of nine squares superimposed over your viewfinder. The secret is to frame up your images so that the main point of focus lands on one of the grid lines. This will create balance in your shots. Try it. And start looking at photos you like, with this rule in mind. I bet most of the ones that stand out for you follow the rule of nine, whether the photographer intended it or not. Check out the end of this chapter for link to a page where you can download more images to match the effects I'm talking about.

Subtle Patterns

Watching out for and using subtle patterns can add another level of rockstar quality to your videos. For example, symmetry in photography creates a powerful visual impact that's both appealing and intriguing. I like to use the vertical lines found in landscapes, doors, architecture, the way people stand, the line of a wall, or even shapes on a table to add interest to a shot.

There are subtle patterns everywhere you look. Once you open up your mind to looking for them, you'll start to see them everywhere: in gardens, wood textures, in the lines of a jetty or a walkway, and in the way people hold objects.

The next time you're outside, see if you can line the shot up with an invisible pattern when you take your next photo. It could be two wall edges lined up together, the edge of a swimming pool with the horizon in the background, or a couple of beach balls on a beach. See what you can come up with. Even the way animals stand or lie can be a pattern that offers a unique perspective to include in your video.

To see images that can help you visualise what I'm talking about here, go to girldirector.com/CameraStyles.

Silhouettes

You'll find silhouettes in nearly everything we do. It's a little bit of a trademark technique for us. I *love* silhouettes. They can help you create mystery, drama, style, and mood in your photos and videos. To take a silhouette shot, place your subject in front of a light source. It could be a sunset, a bright white background, or some other source. As a result, your subject will appear to be dark.

Turn off your flash before you shoot. For an effective silhouette, your subject needs to be dark and the background needs to be light.

The best thing to do is choose something that is an interesting shape as your subject. Some things won't come out as well as others for a silhouette. Think about the shape and about what you want to create.

Have a look at the framing to make sure you're in the best position for the shot, and make sure the image is uncluttered and simple. When you're starting to work with silhouettes, focus on one person, one animal, or one object at a time against the bright background.

Get on the Ground

To create low-angle shots, get down and shoot upwards from beneath the subject. This may mean lying on the ground or crouching really low. You'll often see me lying on the ground when I'm shooting. I love this perspective. It gives you another point of view. Getting down on the ground also means you don't need a tripod, as you can balance the camera on the ground. This is also a good place from which to shoot some foreground stuff.

Filming women from below isn't usually very flattering, as it can make subjects look wider than they really are. If you're shorter, though, it can give you a more powerful look. Play around and keep these tips in mind. Develop your eye. When photographing someone else, always ask yourself if the image you're getting from the angle you're shooting from is one that you'd like of yourself.

Black and White

Everyone looks great in black and white; don't you think? Black and white shots can be used for emotion, for a classic video, or for a number of other reasons. The best black and white photos are based on heavy-contrast shots. If you've taken video or photos in the middle of the day with harsh shadows, the chances are the shots will lend themselves to being great black and white shots (which you can use your computer software to achieve).

When it comes to black-and-white imagery, being able to 'see' how your final shot will look is a key skill. It's important to try to translate the colour image you see through your camera's viewfinder into a monochrome image. To get the best results with black and white, you have to look beyond the colours and try to visualize how a shot's shapes, textures, and tones will be recorded.

Reflections

Using reflections is another creative element to include when you're shooting photographs or video. Including windows, puddles of water, or tide pools – anything that's giving a reflection – can be very dynamic. Reflections are everywhere. Have a look at the close-up of someone's eye or the side of the toaster in the kitchen. See what you can add to your next video and photos by adding reflections.

. . .

BETTER VIDEOS

Objects

You can have lots of fun shooting things instead of people. Or maybe you have products that you want to film properly. When shooting your products, make sure you look at and play around with different backgrounds that are plain and don't take attention away from your product. For example, if you're filming jewellery, look for interesting items to place in the shot with the jewellery that match your brand and your style. Maybe you use nature as your inspiration, including pieces of wood, plants, or leaves to set off your product. Or perhaps you want to use black or white backgrounds so your product stands out.

You can even get great light box setups that are designed specifically for shooting small objects.

Time-lapse

Doing a time-lapse shot is great if you have a scene you want to set up and then leave your camera filming for a period of time. Cameras can be set to only take a shot a few times a second, so that the video seems to move really fast. Time-lapse is perfect for shooting things like clouds, sunsets, flowers opening, and plants growing.

Slow Motion

Get the effect of slow motion by shooting at a faster speed. The resulting video looks slower. It's the exact opposite of time-lapse. For example, when you film something at 5000 frames a second, this creates incredibly slow motion. Standard video is shot at 25 or 30 frames a second, so you can see the difference. iPhones will shoot slow motion at 120 frames a second and faster these days, so have a go at playing with it. I love it. Try jumping in a puddle and filming the water as it splashes.

Blurred Backgrounds

A blurred background is great if you're doing a 'talking head' video (medium close-up shot) with a distracting background. Viewers aren't going to be able to focus on what you're saying if the background is too prominent. That is why it's better to blur out the background of the shot. To do this you need to use a camera that has manual settings; most smartphones won't give you this option.

You need to think about these two things when creating a blurred background:

1. Use a low-aperture setting on the lens. (I usually shoot between f/2.8 and f/3.5).
2. Keep a good distance between the subject and the background.

The best thing I can suggest is to get out there and experiment. It's no good just reading about making videos. You *have* to go out there and play. Have a child-like curiosity about video.

Different Camera Types

Smartphones. You don't need an expensive camera to make great videos. We teach all of our clients to start with a smartphone and learn how to make great videos before they get bogged down in large files. You don't need to spend more money at first in order to understand the basics in making great videos.

DSLR. We find that once our clients have mastered the

smartphone, they want depth in their shots and a more professional finish, so they go to a bigger camera, a DSLR. What I love about a DSLR are the lenses and that it's got manual settings. That's where the power lies with these cameras. You want to learn how to use them in manual mode so you get the best from them. They're perfect for documentaries. In fact, I used a Canon 7D when I went to Thailand. The power of these cameras is in the lens you use. They're so good because you can change lenses and be more creative with what you shoot.

Lenses. The three lenses we suggest having when you have a digital SRL camera are:

1. Zoom lens
2. Wide-angle lens
3. 50 mm lens

I also like to buy old used lenses that have scratches and aren't perfect, because I can get different effects and images and markings. I also use Nikon lenses with my Canon camera. You can get adapters on eBay so that you can use all kinds of lenses on one camera body. The image quality of the shots is based on the lenses, not the body of the camera. Warning: You can spend a fortune on lenses! One cinematographer I worked with on music videos used a $100k lens. I was scared to go near it! But it gave the shots an amazing quality.

Camcorders. Camcorders are great if you're going out and shooting a great deal of footage. They're good for events, like workshops, or for shooting documentaries, because you don't have to focus and worry about lenses.

Watch out about recording too much footage with a camcorder, as it can be very time-consuming afterwards.

. . .

Putting It All Together

After you've done the filming, it's time to put all the elements together and actually create your video. Here are some of the factors to consider.

Motion Design and Effects

This is my favourite subject. I could go on and on about design and effects for a whole book, but I'll just touch on it in here. Design is a silent art and one of the things that will take your videos up a notch.

When you have a logo design or a style, you can create a bunch of design elements in your colours that you can add to your videos. For example, we have our Girl Director logo:

It's a James Bond-style brand with an attitude, and we use it in our videos to make them stand out. We also use a bunch of other elements that represent the Girl Director brand and that fit with our colours and message. If you go to our YouTube channel at youtube.com/girldirectorTV, you can see our shoe that stamps down and has attitude. All by itself, it says a lot about who we are. With that one animation element, we've attracted some of our best clients.

How do you feel about your own brand? What type of movement can you add to your logo? What story can you add to your logo to bring it to life and give it a new dimension? What sounds can bring it to life? Using these and other important design elements will all contribute to making your videos stand out.

The next time you watch TV or YouTube (I know you don't watch TV anymore, but when you do...), watch with a director's eye. Check out different design elements, like when a TV station's logo shows up on screen. Look at the way they use colour and other elements. History is repeating itself. TV quality is now happening online.

Tell a Story with Text

Typography, or text, is another powerful element to use in videos. It's great because it talks to the person watching the video. Sometimes people are unable to watch the video and listen to it while they're at work, for example. If you have text telling part of the story or highlighting certain points, you can create very powerful videos. With this kind of video, music is very important.

Editing

Post-production processing of what you shot is the third stage in the video-making process. The editor role is an important one because once you have all your amazing video shots, it's time to put them together. The editor's job is to make all the pieces of the puzzle come together in one high-WOW-factor video. This includes dealing with the elements of music, graphics, the story, and the flow of the video.

An important editing trick is to remember to use an intro animation of your logo at the very beginning, and to have a call to action at the end of the video, so people know how to find you.

Now is not the time to go into a detailed editing lesson, so I'll tell you that you can make cool videos by editing them on your phone (there are apps that make life easier for you if you have an Android phone). iPhones make it easy. You can use the iMovie app on your iPhone or on your Mac. You can use various programs in editing, like iMovie, Camtasia for basic editing, and Final Cut Pro for Mac. For PCs, there is Sony Movie Studio and Adobe Premiere. There are other, more professional programs, too, but the ones I've listed here are the main ones we suggest. Do a trial download of the software first and use it a bit to see how you like it.

Michael has prepared a short but detailed video about editing on the iPhone that you will love and get so much from. You can watch it here: girldirector.com/iMovieEditing.

If you need your videos edited, make sure you contact us. We have an editing service to help you get your videos out there faster.

Jump Cuts

A jump cut happens when you're editing and put a talking head shot, for example, next to another one from the same set-up but from a disconnected time. It's jarring. It happens when you edit a piece of footage out of the middle and then join the shots from either side. To avoid jump cuts, get enough footage, like adding another camera angle or even using stock footage to help the video flow.

Stock Footage

A good way to get inspiration for developing your technique is to look at stock images. See which ones match the different styles here in the camera techniques section. Then use that idea as inspiration and take action – practice it until you feel that you can create your own magic with that technique.

Connect with People

I always like to connect with the people we're filming. I make time to get to know them, what they're about, and what they love. The best videos I've made were ones where I took the time to really get to know the subjects as part of the shooting process.

Here are my tips for connecting with people before filming:

1. Make them laugh and get them talking about things that are important to them.
2. Tell them how amazing they are – because they are – and mean it.
3. Be honest if you don't like something, like a shooting angle.
4. Follow your instincts.
5. If they feel uncomfortable, a great trick is to just talk to them and say you aren't recording, but record anyway. Often these practice takes are more natural.
6. If the shot isn't working, change it.
7. To make people slimmer, film from slightly above looking down.
8. Play with the position of the camera.
9. Give yourself enough time. At the start of most shoots, the energy can be a little tense. It's like anything – the more time you give yourself beforehand, the better job you'll do, the more relaxed you can be, and the easier and more relaxed the shots will be.

Filming Events

If you want to film your events, the important thing to remember is to use a camera that can record for long periods of time. Generally, DSLR cameras can overheat and are not designed for long periods of time. Canon has great handycam cameras that can do this, but make sure whatever camera you use has an audio input so you can plug in a microphone for better sound.

When shooting an event, set up two cameras: one filming a wider, locked shot and the other doing roaming shots to capture close-up expressions. Many event videos miss those important close-up shots. These are for building emotion and connection in your video. If you shoot everything on a wide lens, you'll lose that deeper connection with your audience.

I find many event videos boring and hard to watch. What can you do to make yours not boring? What can you add, to put something special in your event video? Perhaps tell a story at the start, or tell a story throughout the whole thing, so it's more interesting to watch. Or you could even include some behind-the-scenes shots, or shots of you talking in the empty room before the audience arrives.

Back Up Your Files

Download and back up your shooting files straight away when you're done shooting. Or, even better, as you're shooting. I don't recommend using massive storage flashcards in your camera, in case a whole card fails and you lose the lot. You'd hate to get home and find the flashcard had a fault, which is why it's good to download as you go. Sometimes this isn't possible, which is why a back-up camera comes in handy.

Troubleshooting

Be Prepared. Always have a back-up plan in case things go wrong, such as:

- Rain
- Hard drive may fail

- Camera may fail
- Crew may not show up
- Council may move you on
- Children need a release form signed by parents

Having a second camera that's recording sound as a backup is a great thing to do, because you can always use the soundtrack from one camera and edit it with the images from the other camera, in a worst-case scenario.

Sound. Check to make sure the battery of your microphone is fully charged. Check that the microphone cord is plugged in all the way. Test the sound before shooting. There's nothing worse than doing a great shoot and then finding out that there was no sound recorded. That's infuriating!

Grainy images. The problem is lighting. Generally, grainy images mean you're shooting with poor light conditions. Add more light and the problem is fixed.

Girl Director Secret Technique

Seeing examples will really help you process the techniques above. For visually beautiful images and examples of all of these styles and techniques, go to girldirector.com/CameraStyles.

* * *

My wish for you as you move forward is that you make a difference with videos you were born to make. Create *great* videos, not ordinary ones. Create a movement and make a difference with videos that are aligned with who you are and not with what everyone else is doing. When you find a cause that's big enough and that you feel passionate about, making videos becomes more about them than you. Your passion will keep you going and keep you striving to do more and be more, especially because things will always come up to challenge you. You want something to hold your attention and drive and keep it focused.

I now hand you the baton of the gift of video, so you can go out there and help others. Video is all about the ripple effect. You never know who you're going to help out there.

My intention with this book is for you to be inspired and for you to see what's possible in your life using video. If you have an inner knowing that you're here to do more, and you want to make videos to help others, don't wait! Act on it. You aren't alone. More and more women are stepping up to create powerful videos. There are stories everywhere you look, and now it's your job to communicate them.

A next step I suggest you take is getting in touch with us over at Girl Director HQ. We'd love to hear from you and see what you're making. Our email address is iwantvideos@girldirector.com.

If you get stuck, don't be a stranger! We work with women all over the world, helping them go from not knowing anything about video to being masters. No question is too silly.

Share your successes with us, too. You can tag me on Facebook and connect with us there https://www.facebook.com/GirlDirector/ or subscribe to our YouTube channel (youtube.com/girldirectorTV). We're always adding valuable content to fast track your knowledge. We also have a wonderful video series called Million Dollar Women you will want to study to grow your business.

You are going to love the interactive videos, audio files, and workbook that come with this book. These include camera confidence tools, a bonus style guide for camera work, as well as all kinds of goodies, videos, tools, more tips and techniques, and special things just for you as a reader of this book. If any of the links in this book or on our site don't work for you, tell us, because we may not know if something needs to be changed or fixed.

What you're already doing changes lives. What you're going to be doing with video will change even more lives. I'd be so excited if, even in some small way, this book has contributed to you seeing how beautiful you are on- and off-screen and what you're capable of with video. Video connects you to so much and is such a powerful medium in so many ways. You just never know who's going to be touched by the work you do.

Girl Director Secret Technique

If you want to leave a legacy and create change on the planet, making a documentary or creating a video that creates change is the key. I have a gift of being able to connect to what magic people are meant to create with video. Book a session to find out what you can create: girldirector.com/VSS

THE RIPPLE EFFECT

Have faith that every video you make will create a ripple effect

What does it mean to make a video that has a ripple effect? It means that through your video, your intention, and your marketing, your work touches someone somewhere who you have no idea about. It could be in another country or right next door. Your video has the potential to travel vast distances, to lead to a conversation about an idea that might even change the world. The ripple effect is about the effect one idea can have on people and on other ideas.

Pretty cool, huh?

You are a change-maker. You can make a real difference in the world. If you were drawn to this book, then video is calling to you. Listen to the messages you're receiving. Whether you're being drawn to a documentary that now seems impossible, or an interview, or a music video, or even a corporate video, when you set the right intention the results will be incredibly powerful.

BETTER VIDEOS

Sharing your mission and your message with the world creates change.

Women are coming out into view after being invisible. There's no better time to have a business than now. It's time to push through whatever's holding you back and to clear the way, layer by layer, so you can shine more brightly.

This is all about you being your own director – of your videos, of your life, of the movement you want to start. Just don't let fear and doubt stop you.

We have a mastermind group called The Ripple Effect. We created it especially for women who are change-makers, women who love video and who want to use video to share different ways of thinking; women who are opening up to helping people around the world.

These types of videos can change the world:

1. Video blogs
2. Animal videos
3. Inspiring videos
4. You being you on camera
5. Music videos
6. Documentaries
7. Movies
8. Short films
9. Adverts
10. Educational videos
11. How-to videos
12. Vision board videos

* * *

When creating a documentary or a ripple-effect video, you want to have a good plan. The more you do in the planning process, the better and easier the production will be. With all videos, there are four stages:

1. Pre-production
2. Production
3. Post-production
4. Distribution

The more you can do in the pre-production process, the better your video will be. I've wasted so many hours of my life going out to shoot without having a plan. Please learn from my mistakes and plan first. Your editor will also love you for it.

As I mentioned before, the way I see the future of marketing, it will be more and more about telling stories from the heart, and we'll do it more and more by being involved with organizations that our businesses are aligned with.

The more powerful your marketing videos are, and the more focused they are on your expertise, the more success you have and so the more you can give back and create more videos that change the world. And remember to think big. Although making documentaries takes time and commitment, the rewards are amazing.

All of the videos we've created at Girl Director have had a ripple effect. Some have been music videos that live on and continue to inspire people. Others ripple on through the teachings we offer, so our students can go on and teach others, and so on. It never stops.

This all creates a ripple effect beyond what we can measure.

* * *

BETTER VIDEOS

There are two ripple effect projects I'm really excited about. One is my documentary, *Through Elephant Eyes*, that will create a new awareness about elephants. It's my first documentary. I'm excited about it because it's self-funded. (Girl Director has started putting five percent of the income we receive from our programs into making films that will create a ripple effect.) You can check out what's going on with it on Facebook at facebook.com/ThroughElephantEyes.

The other project I'm excited about is called *Symphony of the Earth*. This is a two-hour, environmental, feature-length film that harnesses the power of music to effect powerful global change. It's a unique film project that empowers humanity to live in harmony with all life on Earth.

We believe the universal language of music can unite the world and inspire action. It's been scientifically proven that sound alone can create structural changes in water molecules. Imagine the global changes sound could create when today's leading musicians unite together on one project?

This project is only in the beginning stages, but we already have some exciting video projects planned to help animals and inspire change on the planet with sound. This will have a massive ripple effect. You can find out more about this project at symphonyoftheearth.org.

I hope you can see that by being a part of amazing video projects, you too can achieve great things. You can create a legacy. Video is getting bigger and bigger. The future will be very different from to what it is today, and video will have been a massive part of the shift that takes place.

Documentaries are the future. The easier the technology gets, the more documentaries and films there will be. Imagine like minds working together to create a ripple effect with the stories they're creating. Your message and your story can open up new ways of thinking. It can educate people and build awareness. What your idea can do is endless. If you have a strong pull toward an idea or a cause, do something about it. The world needs your story.

Girl Director Secret Technique

Talk about your ideas. Get help when you need it. If you're a change-maker and want to create a documentary, or if you have a fantastic idea that you feel is your calling and want to use video. What are you waiting for? girldirector.com/VSS . I will see things you can create beyond what you can see right now.

ACKNOWLEDGMENTS

I want to say a big thank you to my mum and dad for always encouraging me to go after what I wanted in life, no matter how weird or out there my idea was. I felt like I had support, even when they weren't sure how it was all going to turn out. I feel very blessed to have had such creative, free-spirited parents.

A big thank-you to Mum for always being there when it all seemed too much and when I was burnt-out and had no more to give. Thanks to Dad for introducing me to the world of having your own business, for showing me what working hard looks like, and for the experience of working around music. I'm grateful for my brother Amos, who starred in my short film and acted with his friends, and for the countless other times I've reached out to him for support with writing or grammar. His book is next, I'm sure!

Thanks to John and Marcelle, my step-parents, for being there with *huge* support in various ways. And to my little sister, Amalia, who one day may want to carry the Girl Director torch into the future.

A big thank you to Michael for being here and encouraging me and helping me write this book. Your book is *next*! Thanks to Michael's family – Diana, Ralph, Ian, David, Catherine, Natasha, and Olivia – who have put up with me working countless hours on yet another project, and for their patience with me for all those family events I missed by working too much.

Thanks to Jason Hare, who was there for the beginning of my music video-making and is always looking out for me, even today.

Thanks to one of my good friends and mentors, Viv Scanu, who taught me so much about looking through the lens of a camera. I'm grateful for his humbleness and patience as he worked with me on some of my very first music videos and taught me so much about business, life, patience, and cinematography.

Thanks also to another mentor of mine and an inspiration, Emmy and Oscar Awards-winner Dr. Jim Frazier, who has the biggest heart of anyone I've ever met. Jim taught me that anything is possible when you believe in yourself. He also taught me so much about filming nature and wildlife.

Thanks to Peter Flynn, who believed in me when I was at my worst, who encouraged me, pushed me, and really helped me have faith in things again.

Thanks to Nicola Moras, one of my first business mentors. Because of her, I understand the value of always having someone to learn and grow from.

Thanks to Angela Lauria – when I met her and read her book, I knew she was talking to me. She opened up my inner author. One year ago, I had no idea that I even had a book waiting for me to write it. Making a difference is what it's all about.

Thanks to the gorgeous Kerri Chinner, who's an inspiration, showing what this work can do for someone who takes it on to its full capacity. Everything she's done to step up and get where she belongs is just the beginning of her journey.

Thanks to the inspirational diva herself, Helen Sweeney, for trusting in us to help her with her vision and for sticking with it, no matter what came up or got in her way. She is such a bundle of joy and so fun to be around. I can't wait to see what's next for her.

Thanks also to Margaret, Alba, Tara, and Max for letting me share part of their chapters with us. I'm grateful for our clients, every single one of them, for trusting in us to help them through the next part of their journey. We love them and are so grateful to them all. They've all shown and taught us various lessons in various ways.

And, finally, thanks to *you*, for reading this now, for fully embracing what video can do for your life, for being ready to free your inner director, and for setting your creativity free.

ABOUT THE AUTHOR

Rachel Dunn is the founder of Girl Director Academy. She is an expert and leader in video marketing education. Rachel has worked in TV, film, and media for over 30 years as a video director. producer, branding expert, and entrepreneur. She's passionate about finding the hidden stories that need to be told to make the world a better place. She loves to empower and teach companies how to integrate video into their company easily with systems and strategy.

She lives in Queensland with Michael, Girl Director co-director, and their fur baby, Morrison.

Rachel now mentors women to make better videos to stand out, be seen, and attract more clients. She and Michael have helped hundreds of women around the world make better videos and tap into their passion to create videos they love.

Rachel is on the board of directors for the non-profit organization Symphony of the Earth, along with Emmy and Oscar award-winner Dr. Jim Frazier. *Symphony of the Earth* (symphonyoftheearth.org) is a feature film project designed to harness the world's animal sounds and combine them with the sounds of the greatest singers in the world, to inspire change with sound and music by lifting the world's frequency.

In 2021, Rachel is releasing her first documentary, *Through Elephant Eyes*, a film to open minds about animal consciousness, connection, and healing.

In 2011, Rachel spoke to 2500 industry peers about design

and branding at the international event agIdeas International Design Forum, in Melbourne.

Video has opened up so many amazing opportunities. Rachel is passionate about helping others tap into what's possible for them now that the technology is getting easier and easier.

Website: girldirector.com
Email: iwantvideos@girldirector.com

THANK YOU

I would love to see what you're doing now on video. Email me (iwantvideos@girldirector.com) a link to a video of you sharing your passion and, as a special gift, I'll send you a guide on how to always look your best on camera, with personalized tips from me.

Here are more extra-special free goodies for you:

FREE Five-Part How To Make A Video Blog Series
A video series that goes along with this book. You can watch it at
girldirector.com/BetterVideoBlogs

WANT MORE HELP

Are you ready to really to be seen, be noticed, and make better videos?

Sign up for a personal session with so you can see exactly how video will impact your business and help you find amazing, higher-end clients you love.
www.girldirector.com/VSS

www.ingramcontent.com/pod-product-compliance
Lightning Source LLC
Chambersburg PA
CBHW050317010526
44107CB00055B/2286